APPLAUSE FIRST FOLIO EDITIONS

The First Part of Henry the Fourth, with the Life and Death of HENRY Sirnamed HOT-SPURRE

BY

William Shakespeare

PREPARED & ANNOTATED BY

NEIL FREEMAN

APPLAUSE
NEW YORK • LONDON

The Applause Shakespeare Library

Folio Texts

AN APPLAUSE ORIGINAL

The First Part of Henry the Fourth, with the Life and Death of HENRY Sirnamed HOT-SPURRE

original concept devised by Neil Freeman

original research computer entry by Margaret McBride

original software programmes designed and developed by
James McBride and Terry Lim

Text layout designed and executed by Neil Freeman

Some elements of this text were privately published under the collective title of
The Freeman–Nichols Folio Scripts 1991–96

ISBN: 1-55783-417-2

Library of Congress Cataloging-in-Publication Data

Library of Congress Catalog Card Number: 00-103947

British Library Cataloging-in-Publication Data
A catalogue record of this book is available from the British Library

APPLAUSE BOOKS

1841 Broadway Suite 1100
New York, NY 10023
Phone (212) 765-7880
Fax: (212) 765-7875

Combined Book Services Ltd.
Units I/K Paddock Wood Dist. Ctr.
Paddock Wood,
Tonbridge Kent TN12 6UU
Phone 0189 283-7171
Fax 0189 283-7272

Printed in Canada

CONTENTS

GENERAL INTRODUCTION

THE PLAY

APPENDICES

ACKNOWLEDGEMENTS

My grateful thanks to all who have helped in the growth and development of this work. Special thanks to Norman Welsh who first introduced me to the Folio Text, and to Tina Packer who (with Kristin Linklater and all the members of Shakespeare & Co.) allowed me to explore the texts on the rehearsal floor. To Jane Nichols for her enormous generosity in providing the funding which allowed the material to be computerised. To James and Margaret McBride and Terry Lim for their expertise, good humour and hard work. To the National Endowment for the Arts for their award of a Major Artist Fellowship and to York University for their award of the Joseph G. Green Fellowship. To actors, directors and dramaturgs at the Stratford Festival, Ontario; Toronto Free Theatre (that was); the Skylight Theatre, Toronto and Tamanhouse Theatre of Vancouver. To colleagues, friends and students at The University of British Columbia, Vancouver; York University, Toronto; Concordia University, Montreal; The National Theatre School of Canada in Montreal; Equity Showcase Theatre, Toronto; The Centre for Actors Study and Training (C.A.S.T.), Toronto; The National Voice Intensive at Simon Fraser University, Vancouver; Studio 58 of Langara College, Vancouver; Professional Workshops in the Arts, Vancouver; U.C.L.A., Los Angeles; Loyola Marymount, Los Angeles; San Jose State College, California; Long Beach State College, California; Brigham Young University, Utah, and Hawaii; Holy Cross College, Massachussetts; Guilford College, North Carolina. To Chairman John Wright and Associate Dean Don Paterson for their incredible personal support and encouragement. To Rachel Ditor and Tom Scholte for their timely research assistance. To Alan and Chris Baker, and Stephanie McWilliams for typographical advice. To Jay L. Halio, Hugh Richmond, and G.B. Shand for their critical input. To the overworked and underpaid proofreading teams of Ron Oten and Yuuattee Tanipersaud, Patrick Galligan and Leslie Barton, Janet Van De Graaff and Angela Dorhman (with input from Todd Sandomirsky, Bruce Alexander Pitkin, Catelyn Thornton and Michael Roberts). And above all to my wife Julie, for her patient encouragement, courteous advice, critical eye and long sufferance!

SPECIAL ACKNOWLEDGEMENTS

Glenn Young and Paul Sugarman of Applause Books; Houghton Mifflin Company for permission to quote from the line numbering system developed for *The Riverside Shakespeare*: Evans, Gwynne Blakemore, Harry Levin, Anne Barton, Herschel Baker, Frank Kermode, Hallet D. Smith, and Marie Edel, editors, *The Riverside Shakespeare*. Copyright © 1974 by Houghton Mifflin Company.

DEFINITIONS OF AND GUIDE TO PHOTOGRAPHIC COPIES OF THE EARLY TEXTS

(see Appendix A for a brief history of the First Folio, the Quartos, and their uneasy relationship with modern texts)

A QUARTO (Q)

A single text, so called because of the book size resulting from a particular method of printing. Eighteen of Shakespeare's plays were published in this format by different publishers at various dates between 1594–1622 prior to the appearance of the 1623 Folio. Of the eighteen quarto texts, scholars suggest that fourteen have value as source texts. An extremely useful collection of them is to be found in Michael J. B. Allen and Kenneth Muir, eds., *Shakespeare's Plays in Quarto* (Berkeley: University of California Press, 1981).

THE FIRST FOLIO (F1)[1]

Thirty-six of Shakespeare's plays (excluding *Pericles* and *Two Noble Kinsmen,* in which he had a hand) appeared in one volume published in 1623. All books of this size were termed Folios, again because of the sheet size and printing method, hence this volume is referred to as the First Folio; two recent photographic editions of the work are:

Charlton Hinman, ed., *The Norton Facsimile (The First Folio of Shakespeare)* (1968; republished New York: W. W. Norton & Company, Inc., 1996).

Helge Kökeritz, ed., *Mr. William Shakespeare's Comedies, Histories & Tragedies* (New Haven: Yale University Press, 1954).

THE SECOND FOLIO (F2)

Scholars suggest that the Second Folio, dated 1632 but perhaps not published until 1640, has little authority, especially since it created hundreds of new problematical readings of its own. Nevertheless, more than eight hundred modern text readings can be attributed to it. The most recent reproduction is D. S. Brewer, ed., *Mr.*

---

[1] For a full overview of the First Folio see the monumental two-volume work: Charlton Hinman, *The Printing and Proof Reading of the First Folio of Shakespeare* (2 volumes) (Oxford: Clarendon Press, 1963) and W. W. Greg, *The Editorial Problem in Shakespeare: a Survey of the Foundations of the Text,* 3rd. ed. (Oxford: Clarendon Press, 1954); for a brief summary, see the forty-six page publication from Peter W. M. Blayney, *The First Folio of Shakespeare* (Washington, DC: Folger Library Publications, 1991).

William Shakespeare's Comedies, Histories & Tragedies, the Second Folio Repro-
duced in Facsimile (Dover, NH: Boydell & Brewer Ltd., 1985).

The Third Folio (1664) and the Fourth Folio (1685) have even less authority, and
are rarely consulted except in cases of extreme difficulty.

THE THIRD FOLIO (F3)

The Third Folio, carefully proofed (though apparently not against the previous
edition) takes great pains to correct anomalies in punctuation ending speeches and
in expanding abbreviations. It also introduced seven new plays supposedly written
by Shakespeare, only one of which, *Pericles*, has been established as such. The most
recent reproduction is D. S. Brewer, ed., *Mr. William Shakespeare's Comedies, His-*
tories & Tragedies, the Third Folio Reproduced in Facsimile (Dover, NH: Boydell &
Brewer Ltd., 1985).

THE FOURTH FOLIO (F4)

Paradoxically, while the Fourth Folio was the most carefully edited of all, its con-
centration on grammatical clarity and ease of comprehension by its readers at the ex-
pense of faithful reproduction of F1 renders it the least useful for those interested in
the setting down on paper of Elizabethan theatre texts. The most recent reproduction is D. S. Brewer, ed., *Mr. William Shakespeare's Comedies, Histories & Tragedies,*
the Fourth Folio Reproduced in Facsimile (Dover, NH: Boydell & Brewer Ltd., 1985).

WELCOME TO THESE SCRIPTS

These scripts are designed to do three things:

1. show the reader what the First Folio (often referred to as F1) set down on paper, rather than what modern editions think ought to have been set down

2. provide both reader and theatre practitioner an easy journey through some of the information the original readers might have garnered from F1 and other contemporary scripts which is still relevant today

3. provide a simple way for readers to see not only where modern texts alter the First Folio, and how, but also allow readers to explore both First Folio and modern versions of the disputed passage without having to turn to an Appendix or a different text

all this, hopefully without interfering with the action of the play.

What the First Folio sets on paper will be the basis for what you see. In the body of the play-text that follows, the words (including spellings and capitalisations), the punctuation (no matter how ungrammatical), the structure of the lines (including those moments of peculiar verse or unusual prose), the stage directions, the act and scene divisions, and (for the most part) the prefixes used for each character will be as set in the First Folio.

In addition, new, on page, visual symbols specially devised for these texts will help point out both the major stepping stones in the Elizabethan debate/rhetorical process contained in the plays (a fundamental part of understanding both the inner nature of each character as well as the emotional clashes between them), and where and how (and sometimes why) modern texts have altered the First Folio information. And, unlike any other script, opposite each page of text will be a blank page where readers can make their own notes and commentary.

However, there will be the rare occasion when these texts do not exactly follow the First Folio.

Sometimes F1's **words or phrases** are meaningless; for example, the lovely misprinting of 'which' in *Twelfth Night* as 'wh?ch', or in *Romeo and Juliet* the typesetting corruptions of 'speeh' for 'speech' and the running of the two words 'not away' as 'notaway'. If there are no alternative contemporary texts (a Quarto version of the play) or if no modification was made by any of the later Folios (The Second Folio of 1632, The Third Folio of 1664, or The Fourth Folio of 1685, termed F2, F3, and F4 respectively) then the F1 printing will be set as is, no matter how peculiar, and the modern correction footnoted. However, if a more appropriate alternative is available in a Quarto (often referred to as Q) or F2, F3, or F4, that 'correction' will be set directly into the text, replacing the F1 reading, and footnoted accordingly, as in the case of 'wh?ch', 'speeh', and 'notaway'.

The only time F1's **punctuation** will be altered is when the original setting is so blurred that an accurate deciphering of what F1 set cannot be determined. In such cases, alternative punctuation from F2–4 or Q will be set and a footnote will explain why.

The only time F1's **line structure** will not be followed is when at the end of a very long line, the final word or part of the word cannot fit onto the single line, nor be set as a new line in F1 because of the text that follows and is therefore set above or below the original line at the right hand side of the column. In such rare cases these texts will complete the line as a single line, and mark it with a † to show the change from F1. In all other cases, even when in prose F1 is forced to split the final word of a speech in half, and set only a few letters of it on a new line—for example in *Henry the Fifth*, Pistoll's name is split as 'Pi' on one line and 'stoll' (as the last part of the speech) on the next—these texts will show F1 exactly as set.

Some liberties have to be taken with the **prefixes** (the names used at the beginning of speeches to show the reader which character is now speaking), for Ff (all the Folios) and Qq (all the Quartos) are not always consistent. Sometimes slightly different abbreviations are used for the same character—in *The Tempest,* King Alonso is variously referred to as 'Al.', 'Alo.', 'Alon.', and 'Alonso'. Sometimes the same abbreviation is used for two different characters—in *A Midsummer Nights Dream* the characters Quince, the 'director' and author of the Mechanicals play, and Titania, Queen of the fairies, are given the same abbreviation 'Qu.'. While in this play common sense can distinguish what is intended, the confusions in *Julius Caesar* between Lucius and Lucullus, each referred to sometimes as 'Luc.', and in *The Comedy of Errors,* where the twin brothers Antipholus are both abbreviated to 'Antiph.', cannot be so easily sorted out. Thus, whereas F1 will show a variety of abbreviated prefixes, these texts will usually choose just one complete name per character and stay with it throughout.

However, there are certain cases where one full name will not suffice. Sometimes F1 will change the prefix for a single character from scene to scene, the change usually reflecting the character's new function or status. Thus in *The Comedy of Errors,* as a drinking companion of the local Antipholus, the goldsmith Angelo is referred to by his given name 'Ang.', but once business matters go awry he very quickly becomes a businessman, referred to as 'Gold'. Similar changes affect most of the characters in *A Midsummer Nights Dream,* and a complex example can be found in *Romeo and Juliet.* While modern texts give Juliet's mother the single prefix Lady Capulet throughout (incorrectly since neither she nor Capulet are named as aristocrats anywhere in the play) both Ff and Qq refer to her in a wonderful character-revealing multiplicity of ways—Mother, Capulet Wife, Lady, and Old Lady—a splendid gift for actress, director, designer, and reader alike.

Surprisingly, no modern text ever sets any of these variations. Believing such changes integral to the development of the characters so affected, these texts will. In such cases, each time the character's prefix changes the new prefix will be set, and a small notation alongside the prefix (either by reference to the old name, or by adding the symbol •) will remind the reader to whom it refers.

Also, some alterations will be made to F1's **stage directions,** not to the words themselves or when they occur, but to the way they are going to be presented visually. Scholars agree F1 contains two different types of stage direction: those that came in the original manuscript from which the Playhouse copy of the play was made, and a second set that were added in for theatrical clarification by the Playhouse. The scholars conjecture that the literary or manuscript directions, presumably from Shakespeare, mainly dealing with entries and key actions such as battles, are those that F1 sets centred on a separate line, while the additional Playhouse directions, usually dealing with offstage sounds, music, and exits, are those F1 sets alongside the spoken dialogue, usually flush against the right hand side of the column. In performance terms there seems to be a useful distinction between the two, though this is only a rule of thumb. The centred manuscript (Shakespearean?) directions tend to stop or change the action of the play, that is, the scene is affected by the action the direction demands, whereas the Playhouse directions (to the side of the text) serve to underscore what is already taking place. (If a word is needed to distinguish the two, the centred directions can be called 'action' directions, because they are events in and of themselves, while the side-set directions could be called 'supportive' or 'continuous' since they tend not to distract from the current onstage action.)

Since F1 seems to visually distinguish between the two types (setting them on different parts of the page) and there seems to be a logical theatrical differentiation as to both the source and function of each, it seems only appropriate that these scripts also mark the difference between them. Both Ff and Qq's side-set directions are often difficult to decipher while reading the text: sometimes they are set so close to the spoken text they get muddled up with it, despite the different typeface, and oftentimes have to be abbreviated to fit in. These are drawbacks shared by most modern texts. Thus these texts will distinguish them in a slightly different way (see p. xxvi below).

Finally, there will be two occasional alterations to Ff's **fonts.** F1 used **italics** for a large number of different purposes, sometimes creating confusion on the page. What these texts will keep as italics are letters, poems, songs, and the use of foreign languages. What they will not set in italics are real names, prefixes, and stage directions. Also at the top of each play, and sometimes at the beginning of a letter or poem, F1 would set a large wonderfully **decorative opening letter,** with the second letter of the word being capitalised, the style tying in with the borders that surrounded the opening and closing of each play. Since these texts will not be reproducing the decorative borders, the decorative letters won't be set either.

MAKING FULL USE OF THESE TEXTS

WHAT MODERN CHANGES WILL BE SHOWN

WORDS AND PHRASES

Modern texts often tidy up F1's words and phrases. Real names, both of people and places, and foreign languages are often reworked for modern understanding; for example, the French town often set in F1 as 'Callice' is usually reset as 'Calais'. Modern texts 'correct' the occasional Elizabethan practice of setting a singular noun with plural verb (and vice versa), as well as the infrequent use of the past tense of a verb to describe a current situation. These texts will set the F1 reading, and footnote the modern corrections whenever they occur.

More problematical are the possibilities of choice, especially when a Q and F version of the same play show a different reading for the same line and either choice is valid—even more so when both versions are offered by different modern texts. Juliet's 'When I shall die,/Take him and cut him out in little starres' offered by Ff/Q1-3 being offset by Q4's 'When he shall die...' is a case in point. Again, these texts will set the F1 reading, and footnote the alternatives.

LINE STRUCTURE CHANGES RELATED TO PROBLEMS OF 'CASTING-OFF'

The First Folio was usually prepared in blocks of twelve pages at a time. Six pairs of pages would be prepared, working both forward and backward simultaneously. Thus from the centre of any twelve-page block, pages six and seven were set first, then five and eight, then four and nine, then three and ten, then two and eleven, and finally one and twelve. This meant each compositor had to work out very carefully how much copy would fit not only each sheet, but also how much would be needed overall to reach the outer edges of pages one and twelve to match it to the previously set text, (prior to page one) or about to be set text (after page twelve). Naturally the calculations weren't always accurate. Sometimes there was too little text left for too great a space: in such cases, if the manuscript were set as it should have been, a great deal of empty paper would be left free, a condition often described as 'white' space. Sometimes too much text remained for too small a space, and if the manuscript were to be set according to its normal layout, every available inch would be taken up with type (and even then the text might not fit), a condition that could be described as 'crammed space'.

Essentially, this created a huge design problem, and most commentators suggest when it arose the printing house policy was to sacrifice textual accuracy to neatness of design. Thus, so the argument goes, in the case of white space, extra lines of type would have to be created where (presumably) none originally existed. *Hamlet* provides an excellent example with the Polonius speech 'Indeed that's out of the air' starting at line 78 of what most modern texts term Act Two Scene 2. Q2 sets the four-line speech as prose, and most modern texts follow suit. However, F1, faced with a potentially huge white space problem at the bottom of the right hand column of p. 261 in the Tragedy section, resets the speech as eleven lines of very irregular verse! In the case of crammed space, five lines of verse might suddenly become three lines of prose, or in one very severe case of overcrowding in *Henry The Fourth Part Two*, words, phrases, and even half lines of text might be omitted to reduce the text sufficiently.

When such cases occur, this text will set F1 as shown, and the modern texts' suggested alternatives will be footnoted and discussed.

LINE STRUCTURE CHANGES NOT RELATED TO PROBLEMS OF 'CASTING-OFF'

In addition, modern texts regularly make changes to F1's line structure which are not related to 'white' or 'crammed' space, often to the detriment of both character and scene. Two major reasons are offered for the changes.

First, either (a few) prose lines suddenly appear in what essentially is a verse scene (or a few verse lines in a sea of prose) and the modern texts, feeling the scene should be standardised, restructure the offending lines accordingly. *The Tempest* is atrociously served this way[2], for where F1, the only source text, shows the conspirators Caliban, Stephano, and, very occasionally, Trinculo, speaking verse as well as prose even within the same speech (a sure sign of personal striving and inner disturbance) most modern texts readjust the lines to show only Caliban speaking verse (dignifying him more than he deserves) and Stephano and Trinculo only speaking prose (thus robbing them of their dangerous flights of fancy).

Second, some Ff verse lines appear so appallingly defective in terms of their rhythm and length that modern texts feel it necessary to make a few 'readjustments' of the lines around them to bring the offending lines back to a coherent, rhythmic whole. Many of the later plays are abominably served in this regard: in *Macbeth*, for example, over a hundred F1 passages involving more than 200 lines (90 percent of which were set by the usually reliable compositor A) have been altered by most modern texts. Most of these changes concentrate on regularising moments where a character is under tremendous upheaval and hardly likely to be speaking pure formal verse at that particular moment!

These changes come about through a mistaken application of modern grammat-

---

[2] Commentators suggest the copy play used for setting F1, coming from Stratford as it did, and thus unsupervised by Shakespeare in the Playhouse preparation of the document, prepared by Ralph Crane, was at times defective, especially in distinguishing clearly between verse and prose: this is why most modern texts do not follow F1's choices in these dubious passages: readers are invited to explore *The Tempest* within this series, especially the footnotes, as a theatrical vindication of the original F1 setting

ical considerations to texts that were originally prepared not according to grammar but rhetoric. One of rhetoric's many strengths is that it can show not only when characters are in self-control but also when they are not. In a rhetorically set passage, the splutters of a person going through an emotional breakdown, as with Othello, can be shown almost verbatim, with peculiar punctuations, spellings, breaks, and all. If the same passage were to be set grammatically it would be very difficult to show the same degree of personal disintegration on the printed page.[3] F1's occasional weird shifts between verse and prose and back again, together with the moments of extreme linear breakdown, are the equivalents of human emotional breakdown, and once the anomalies of Elizabethan script preparation are accounted for,[4] the rhetorical breakdowns on F1's printed page are clear indications of a character's disintegration within the play. When modern texts tidy up such blemishes grammatically they unwittingly remove essential theatrical and/or character clues for reader and theatre person alike.

In these texts, F1's line structure will be set as is, and all such modern alterations (prose to verse, verse to prose, regularisation of originally unmetrical lines) will be shown. The small symbol ° will be added to show where modern texts suggest a line should end rather than where F1 shows it does. A thin vertical line will be set to the left alongside any text where the modern texts have converted F1's prose to verse, or vice versa. The more large-scale of these changes will be boxed for quicker reader recognition. Most of these changes will be footnoted in the text where they occur, and a comparison of the two different versions of the text and what each could signify theatrically will be offered. For examples of both, see p. xxiii below.

THE SPECIAL PROBLEMS AFFECTING WHAT ARE KNOWN AS 'SHARED' OR 'SPLIT' VERSE LINES

A definition, and their importance to the Shakespeare texts

Essentially, split lines are short lines of verse which, when placed together, form the equivalent of a full verse line. Most commentators suggest they are very useful in speeding the play along, for the second character (whose line attaches on to the end of the first short line) is expected to use the end of the first character's line as a

---

[3] For a full discussion of this, readers are directed to Neil Freeman, *Shakespeare's First Texts* (Vancouver: Folio Scripts, 1994).

[4] Readers are referred to an excellent chapter by Gary Taylor which analyses the whole background, conjectured and known, concerning the preparation of the first scripts. He points out the pitfalls of assuming the early texts as sole authority for all things Shakespearean: he examines the conjectured movement of the scripts from Shakespeare's pen to printed edition, and carefully examples the changes and alterations that could occur, (most notably at the hands of the manuscript copyists), as well as the interferences and revampings of the Playhouse, plus the effects of the first typesetters' personal habits and carelessness. Stanley Wells and Gary Taylor, *William Shakespeare: A Textual Companion* (Oxford: Clarendon Press, 1987), 1–68.

springboard and jump in with an immediate reply, enhancing the quickness of the debate. Thus in *Measure for Measure*, Act Two Scene 2, modern ll. 8–10, the Provost, trying to delay Claudio's execution, has asked Angelo whether Claudio has to die the following day: Angelo's questioning affirmation ends with a very pointed short line, followed immediately by a short line opening from the Provost.

Angelo	Did I not tell thee yea? hadst thou not order? Why do'st thou aske againe?
Provost	Lest I might be too rash: Under your good correction, I have seene When after execution...

If the Provost replies immediately after, or just as, Angelo finishes, an explosive dramatic tension is created. Allowing a minor delay before reply, as many actors do, will reduce the impact of the moment, and create a hesitation where one probably does not exist.

The occasional problem

So far so good. But the problems start when more than two short lines follow each other. If there are three short lines in succession, which should be joined, #1 and #2, or #2 and #3? Later in the same scene, Claudio's sister Isabella has, at the insistence of Claudio's friend Lucio, come to plead with Angelo for her brother's life. In Lucio's eyes she is giving up too easily, hence the following (modern ll. 45–49):

Lucio	You are too cold: if you should need a pin, You could not with more tame a tongue desire it: To him, I say.
Isabella	Must he needs die?
Angelo	Maiden, no remedie?

And here it seems fairly obvious Isabella and Angelo's lines should join together, thus allowing a wonderful dramatic pause following Lucio's urging before Isabella plucks up enough courage to try. Most modern texts set the lines accordingly, with Lucio's the short odd line out.

But what about the three lines contained in the exchange that follows almost straightaway?

Isabella	But you might doe't & do the world no wrong If so your heart were touch'd with that remorse, As mine is to him?
Angelo	Hee's sentenc'd, tis too late.
Lucio	You are too cold.
Isabella	Too late? why no: I that doe speak a word

> May call it againe: well, beleeve this
> (modern line numbering 53–56)

Does Angelo's 'Hee's sentenc'd...' spring off Isabella's line, leaving Isabella speechless and turning to go before Lucio urges her on again? Or does Angelo pause (to frame a reply?) before speaking, leaving Lucio to quickly jump in quietly giving Isabella no time to back off? Either choice is possible, and dramatically valid. And readers should be allowed to make their own choice, which automatically means each reader should able to see the possibility of such choices when they occur.

The problem magnified by the way modern texts set split/shared lines

However, because of a peculiarity faced by the modern texts not shared by Ff/Qq, modern texts rarely show such possibilities to their readers but make the choice for them. The peculiarity comes about from a change in text layout initiated in the eighteenth century.

Ff/Qq always set short lines directly under one another, as shown in the examples above. In 1778 George Steevens, a highly respected editor, started to show split lines a new way, by advancing the second split line to just beyond where the first split line finishes, viz.

Angelo	Did I not tell thee yea? hadst thou not order?
	Why do'st thou aske againe?
Provost	Lest I might be too rash:
	Under your good correction, I have seene
	When after execution...

Since that date all editions of Shakespeare have followed this practice, which is fine as long as there are only two short lines, but when three follow each other, a choice has to be made. Thus the second Isabella/Angelo/Lucio sequence could be set as either

Isabella	But you might doe't & do the world no wrong
	If so your heart were touch'd with that remorse,
	As mine is to him?
Angelo	Hee's sentenc'd, tis too late.
Lucio	You are too cold.
Isabella	Too late? why no: I that doe speak a word
	May call it againe: well, beleeve this...

(the usual modern choice), or

Isabella	But you might doe't & do the world no wrong
	If so your heart were touch'd with that remorse,
	As mine is to him?

Angelo	Hee's sentenc'd, tis too late.
Lucio	You are too cold.
Isabella	Too late? why no: I that doe speak a word May call it againe: well, beleeve this . . .

This modern typesetting convention has robbed the reader of a very important moment of choice. Indeed, at the beginning of the twentieth century, Richard Flatter[5] suggested that what modern commentators consider to be split lines may not be split lines at all. He offers two other suggestions: pauses and hesitations could exist between each line, or the lines could in fact be spoken one on top of another, a very important consideration for the crowd responses to Anthony in the funeral scene of *Julius Caesar*. Either way, the universally adopted Steevens layout precludes the reader/theatre practitioner from even seeing such possibilities.

These texts will show the F1 layout as is, and will indicate via footnote when a choice is possible (in the case of three short lines, or more, in succession) and by the symbol } when the possibility of springboarding exists. Thus the Folio Texts would show the first Angelo/Provost example as:

Angelo	Did I not tell thee yea? hadst thou not order? Why do'st thou aske againe?
Provost	Lest I might be too rash: } Under your good correction, I have seene When after execution . . .

In nearly all cases the } shows where most modern texts insist on setting a shared split line. However, readers are cautioned that in many of the later plays, the single line so created is much longer than pentameter, and often very a-rhythmic. In such cases the lines could have great value as originally set (two separate short lines), especially when a key debate is in process (for example, *Measure for Measure, The Tragedie of Cymbeline, Othello,* and *The Winters Tale*).

THE UNUSUAL SINGLE SPLIT LINE (PLEASE SEE 'A CAVEAT', P. XXXVIII)

So far the discussion has centred on short lines shared by two or more characters. Ff/Qq offer another complication rarely, if ever, accepted by most modern texts. Quite often, and not because of white space, a single character will be given two consecutive short lines within a single speech. *Romeo and Juliet* is chock full of this device: in the famous balcony scene (modern texts numbering 2.2.62–3) Juliet asks Romeo

How cam'st thou hither.

---

[5]   Richard Flatter, *Shakespeare's Producing Hand* (London: Heinemann, 1948, reprint).

Tell me, and wherefore?
The Orchard walls are high, and hard to climbe

The first two lines (five syllables each) suggest a minute pause between them as Juliet hesitates before asking the all important second line (with its key second part 'and wherefore'). Since Qq rarely set such 'single split lines' most modern texts refuse to set any of them, but combine them:

How cams't thou hither. Tell me and wherefore?

This basically F1 device is set by all the compositors and followed by all other Folios. This text will follow suit, highlighting them with the symbol → for quick recognition, viz.:

How cam'st thou hither. →
Tell me, and wherefore?
The Orchard walls are high, and hard to climbe

SENTENCE AND PUNCTUATION STRUCTURES

A CHARACTER'S THOUGHTFUL & EMOTIONAL JOURNEY

A quick comparison between these texts and both the Ff/Qq's and the modern texts will reveal two key differences in the layout of the dialogue on the printed page — the bolding of major punctuation, and the single line dropping of text whenever a new sentence begins.

The underlying principle behind these texts is that since the handwritten documents from which they stem were originally intended for the actor and Playhouse, in addition to their poetical values, the Ff/Qq scripts represent a theatrical process. Even if the scripts are being read just for pleasure, at the back of the reader's mind should be the notion of characters on a stage and actors acting (and the word 'process' rather than 'practice' is deliberate, with process suggesting a progression, development, or journey).

The late Jean-Louis Barrault gave a wonderful definition of acting, and of this journey, suggesting an actor's job was to strive to remain in 'the ever-changing present'. If something happens onstage (an entry, an exit, a verbal acceptance or denial of what the actor's character has suggested), the 'present' has changed, and the character must readjust accordingly. Just as onstage, the actor should be prepared for the character to re-adjust, and in rehearsal should be examining how and why it does, so should the reader in the library, armchair, or classroom.

In many ways, the key to Shakespeare is discovering how each character's mind works; perceiving the emotions and intellects as they act and react helps the reader understand from where the poetical imagination and utterance stem.

Certain elements of each character's emotional and intellectual journey, and where it changes, are encoded into the sentence structure of Ff/Qq.

Elizabethan education prepared any schooled individual (via the 'petty school' and the private tutor) for the all important and essential daily rough and tumble of argument and debate. Children were trained not only how to frame an argument so as to win it hands down, but also how to make it entertaining so as to enthrall the neutral listener.

The overall training, known as 'rhetoric', essentially allowed intellect and emotion to exist side by side, encouraging the intellect to keep the emotion in check. The idea was not to deny the emotions, but ensure they didn't swamp the 'divinity' of reason, the only thing separating man from beast. While the initial training was mainly vocal, any written matter of the period automatically reflected the ebb and flow of debate. What was set on the printed page was not grammar, but a representation of the rhetorical process.

DROPPING A LINE TO ILLUSTRATE F1'S SENTENCE STRUCTURE

Put at its simplest, in any document of the period, each sentence would represent a new intellectual and emotional stage of a rhetorical argument. When this stage of the argument was completed, a period would be set (occasionally a question mark or, much more rarely, an exclamation mark—both followed by a capital letter) signifying the end of that stage of the argument, and the beginning of the next.

Thus in the First Folio, the identification of each new sentence is an automatic (and for us, four hundred years later, a wonderful) aid to understanding how a character is reacting to and dealing with Barrault's ever-changing present.

To help the reader quickly spot the new steppingstone in an argument, and thus the point of transition, these texts highlight where one sentence ends and the new one begins by simply dropping a line whenever a new sentence starts. Thus the reader has a visual reminder that the character is making a transition to deal with a change in the current circumstances of the scene (or in the process of self-discovery in the case of soliloquies).

This device has several advantages. The reader can instantly see where the next step in the argument begins. The patterns so created on the page can quickly illuminate whenever a contrast between characters' thought patterns occurs. (Sometimes the sentences are short and precise, suggesting the character is moving quickly from one idea to the next. Sometimes the sentences are very long, suggesting the character is undergoing a very convoluted process. Sometimes the sentences contain nothing but facts, suggesting the character has no time to entertain; sometimes they are filled with high-flown imagery, perhaps suggesting the character is trying to mask a very weak argument with verbal flummery.) The patterns can also show when a character's style changes within itself, say from long and convoluted to short and precise, or vice versa. It can also immediately pinpoint when a character is in trouble and not arguing coherently or logically, something modern texts often alter out of grammatical necessity.

With patience, all this could be gleaned from the modern texts (in as far as they set the Ff sentence structure, which they often don't) and from a photostat of the First Folio, by paying special attention to where the periods are set. But there is one extra very special advantage to this new device of dropping a line: this has to do once more with the Elizabethan method of setting down spoken argument on paper, especially when the character speaking is not in the best of all possible worlds.

If an Elizabethan person/character is arguing well, neatly, cleanly, tidily, then a printed representation of that argument would also be clean, neat, and tidy—to modern eyes it would be grammatically acceptable. If the same character is emotionally upset, or incapable of making a clear and tidy argument, then the on-paper representation would be muddy and untidy—to modern eyes totally ungrammatical and often not acceptable. By slightly isolating each sentence these texts very quickly allow the reader to spot when a sentence's construction is not all that it should be, say in the middle of Viola's so-called ring speech in *Twelfth Night* (Act Two Scene 2), or Helena's declaration of love for Bertram in *All's Well That Ends Well* (Act One Scene 3), or the amazing opening to *As You Like It,* where Orlando's opening litany of complaint against his brother starts with a single sentence twenty lines long.

This is especially relevant when a surprising modern editorial practice is accounted for. Very often the Ff sentence structures are markedly altered by modern texts, especially when the Ff sentences do not seem 'grammatical'—thus Orlando's twenty-line monster is split into six separate, grammatically correct sentences by all modern texts. And then there is the case of Shylock in *The Merchant of Venice,* a Jewish man being goaded and tormented beyond belief by the very Christians who helped his daughter elope with a Christian, taking a large part of Shylock's fortune with her. A sentence comparison of the famous Act Three Scene 1 speech culminating in 'Hath not a Jew eyes?' is very instructive. All modern texts set the speech as between fifteen and seventeen sentences in length: whatever the pain, anger, and personal passion, the modern texts encourage dignity and self-control, a rational Shylock. But this is a Shylock completely foreign to both Q1 and Ff. Q1 show the same speech as only four sentences long, Ff five—a veritable onflow of intellect and passion all mixed together, all unstoppable for the longest period of time—a totally different being from that shown by the modern texts. What is more, this is a totally different Shylock from the one seen earlier in the Ff/Q1 version of the play, where, even in the extremes of discomfort with the old enemy Anthonio, his sentence structures are rhetorically balanced and still grammatical to modern eyes.

Here, with Shylock, there are at least three benefits to dropping the sentence: the unusualness of the speech is immediately spotted; the change in style between this and any of his previous speeches can be quickly seen; and, above all, the moment where the speech moves from a long unchecked outpouring to a quick series of brief, dangerously rational sentences can be quickly identified. And these advantages will be seen in such changed sentence circumstances in any play in any of these texts.

THE HIGHLIGHTING OF THE MAJOR PUNCTUATION IN THESE TEXTS

A second key element of rhetoric encoded into the Ff/Qq texts clearly shows the characters' mind in action. The encoding lies in the remaining punctuation which, unlike much modern punctuation, serves a double function, one dealing with the formation of the thought, the other with the speaking of it.

Apart from the period, dealt with already, essentially there are two sets of punctuation to consider, minor and major, each with their own very specific functions.

Shakespearean characters reflect the mode of thinking of their time. Elizabethans were trained to constantly add to or modify thoughts. They added a thought to expand the one already made. They denied the first thought so as to set up alternatives. They elaborated a thought so as to clarify what has already been said. They suddenly moved into splendid puns or non-sequiturs (emotional, logical, or both) because they had been immediately stimulated by what they or others had just said. The **minor punctuation** (essentially the comma [,] the parenthesis or bracket [( )], and the dash) reflects all this.

In establishing thought processes for each character, minor punctuation shows every new nuance of thought: every tiny punctuation in this category helps establish the deftness and dance of each character's mind. In *As You Like It* (Act Three Scene 2, modern line numbering 400–402) the Ff setting of Rosalind's playing with her beloved Orlando has a wonderful coltish exuberance as she runs rings round his protestations of love:

> Love is meerely a madnesse, and I tel you,
> deserves as well a darke house,* and a whip,* as madmen do:

Her mind is adding extra thoughts as she goes: the Ff commas are as much part of her spirit and character as the words are—though most modern texts create a much more direct essayist, preaching what she already knows, by removing the two Ff commas marked *.[6]

A similar situation exists with Macbeth, facing Duncan whom he must kill if he is

---

[6] Unfortunately, many modern texts eradicate the F and Q minor punctuation arguing the need for light (or infrequent) punctuation to preserve the speed of speech. This is not necessarily helpful, since what it removes is just a new thought marker, not an automatic indication to pause: too often the result is that what the first texts offer a character as a series of closely-worked out dancing thought-patterns (building one quick thought—as marked by a comma—on top of another) is turned into a series of much longer phrases: often, involved and reactive busy minds are artificially turned into (at best) eloquent ones, suddenly capable of perfect and lengthy rationality where the situation does not warrant such a reaction, or (at worst) vapid ones, speaking an almost preconceived essay of commentary or artificial sentimentality.

to become king (Act One Scene 4, modern line numbering 22–27). Ff show a Macbeth almost swamped with extra thoughts as he assures Duncan

> The service,* and the loyaltie I owe,
> In doing it,* payes it selfe.
> Your highnesse part,* is to receive our Duties,
> And our Duties are to your Throne,* and State,
> Children,* and Servants; which doe but what they should,*
> By doing every thing safe toward your Love
> And Honour.

The heavy use of minor punctuation—especially when compared with most modern texts which remove the commas marked *, leaving Macbeth with just six thoughts compared to Ff's twelve—clearly shows a man ill at ease and/or working too hard to say the right thing. Again the punctuation helps create an understanding of the character.

However, while the minor punctuation is extremely important in the discovery process of reading and/or rehearsal, paradoxically, it mustn't become too dominant. From the performance/speaking viewpoint, to pause at each comma would be tantamount to disaster. There would be an enormous dampening effect if reader/actor were to pause at every single piece of punctuation: the poetry would be destroyed and the event would become interminable.

In many ways, minor punctuation is the Victorian child of Shakespearean texts, it must be seen but not heard. (In speaking the text, the new thought the minor punctuation represents can be added without pausing: a change in timbre, rhythm, or pitch—in acting terms, occurring naturally with changes in intention—will do the trick.)

But once thoughts have been discovered, they have to be organised into some form of coherent whole. If the period shows the end of one world and the start of the new, and if the comma marks a series of small, ever-changing, ever-evolving thoughts within each world, occasionally there must be pause for reflection somewhere in the helter-skelter of tumbling new ideas. This is the **major punctuation's** strength; major punctuation consisting of the semicolon [;], and the colon [:].

Major punctuation marks the gathering together of a series of small thoughts within an overall idea before moving onto something new. If a room full of Rodin sculptures were analogous to an Elizabethan scene or act, each individual piece of sculpture would be a speech, the torso or back or each major limb a separate sentence. Each collective body part (a hand, the wrist, the forearm, the upper arm) would be a series of small thoughts bounded by major punctuation, each smaller item within that part (a finger, a fingernail, a knuckle) a single small thought separated by commas. In describing the sculpture to a friend one might move from the smaller details (the knuckle) to the larger (the hand) to another larger (the wrist) then another (the forearm) and so on to the whole limb. Unless the speaker is emotionally moved by the recollection, some pauses would be essential, certainly after finishing the whole description of the arm (the sentence), and probably after each major collective of the hand, the wrist, etc. (as marked by the major punctuation), but not after every small bit.

As a rule of thumb, and simply stated, the colon and semicolon mark both a thinking and a speaking pause. The vital difference between major and minor punctuation, whether in the silent reading of the text or the performing of it aloud, is you need not pause at the comma, bracket, or dash; you probably should at the colon, semicolon, and period.

Why the Major Punctuation is Bolded in These Texts.

In speaking the text or reading it, the minor punctuation indicates the need to key onto the new thought without necessarily requiring a pause. In so doing, the inherent rhythms of speech, scene, and play can clip along at the rate suggested by the Prologue in *Romeo and Juliet*, 'the two hours traffic of the stage', until a pause is absolutely necessary. Leave the commas alone, and the necessary pauses will make themselves known.

The 'major' punctuation then comes into its own, demanding double attention as both a thinking and speaking device. This is why it is bolded, to highlight it for the reader's easier access. The reader can still use all the punctuation when desired, working through the speech thought by thought, taking into account both major and minor punctuation as normal. Then, when needed, the bolding of the major punctuation will allow the reader easy access for marking where the speech, scene, or play needs to be broken down into its larger thinking/speaking (and even breathing) units without affecting its overall flow.

The Blank Pages Within the Text

In each text within this series, once readers reach the play itself they will find that with each pair of pages the dialogue is printed on the right-hand page only. The left-hand page has been deliberately left blank so that readers, actors, directors, stage managers, teachers, etc. have ample space for whatever notes and text emendations they may wish to add.

PRACTICAL ON-PAGE HELP FOR THE READER

THE VISUAL SYMBOLS HIGHLIGHTING MODERN ALTERATIONS

THE BOX

This surrounds a passage where the modern texts have made whole-scale alterations to the Ff text. Each boxed section will be footnoted, and the changes analysed at the bottom of the page.

THE FOOTNOTES

With many modern texts the footnotes are not easily accessible. Often no indication is given within the text itself where the problem/choice/correction exists. Readers are forced into a rather cumbersome four-step process. First, they have to search through the bottom of the page where the footnotes are crammed together, often in very small print, to find a line number where an alteration has been made. Then they must read the note to find out what has been altered. Then they must go back to the text and search the side of the page to find the corresponding line number. Having done all this, finally they can search the line to find the word or phrase that has been changed (sometimes complicated by the fact the word in question is set twice in different parts of the line).

These texts will provide a reference marker within the text itself, directly alongside the word or phrase that is in question. This guides the reader directly to the corresponding number in the footnote section of the bottom of each page, to the alteration under discussion—hopefully a much quicker and more immediate process.

In addition, since there are anywhere between 300 and 1,100 footnotes in any one of these texts, a tool is offered to help the reader find only those notes they require, when they require them. In the footnote section, prior to the number that matches the footnote marker in the text, a letter or combination of letters will be set as a code. The letter 'W', for example, shows that the accompanying footnote refers to word substitutions offered by modern texts; the letters 'SD' refer to an added or altered stage direction; the letters 'LS' show the footnote deals with a passage where the modern texts have completely altered the line-structure that F1 set. This enables readers to be selective when they want to examine only certain changes, for they can quickly skim through the body of footnotes until they find the code they want, perhaps those dealing with changes in prefixes (the code 'P') or when modern alterations have been swapping lines from verse to prose or vice versa (the code 'VP'). For full details of the codes, see pp. xxxiii–xxxv below.

Readers are urged to make full use of the footnotes in any of the Recommended Texts listed just before the start of the play. They are excellent in their areas of expertise. To attempt to rival or paraphrase them would be redundant. Thus the footnotes in these scripts will hardly ever deal with word meanings and derivations; social or political history; literary derivations and comparisons; or lengthy quotations from scholars or commentators. Such information is readily available in the *Oxford English Dictionary* and from the recommended modern texts.

Generally, the footnotes in these scripts will deal with matters theatrical and textual and will be confined to three major areas: noting where and how the modern texts alter F1's line structure; showing popular alternative word readings often selected by the modern texts (these scripts will keep the F1 reading unless otherwise noted); and showing the rare occasions where and how these scripts deviate from their source texts. When the modern texts offer alternative words and/or phrases to F2-4/Qq, the original spelling and punctuation will be used. Where appropriate, the footnotes will briefly refer to the excellent research of the scholars of the last three centuries, and to possible theatrical reasons for maintaining F1's structural 'irregularities'.

THE SYMBOL °

This will be used to show where modern texts have altered F1's line structure, and will allow the reader to explore both the F1 setting and the modern alternative while examining the speech where it is set, in its proper context and rightful position within the play. For example, though F1 is usually the source text for *Henry the Fifth* and sets the dialogue for Pistoll in prose, most modern texts use the memorial Q version and change his lines to (at times extraordinarily peculiar) verse. These texts will set the speech as shown in F1, but add the ° to show the modern texts alterations, thus:

> Pistoll   Fortune is Bardolphs foe, and frownes on him:°
> for he hath stolne a Pax, and hanged must a be:° a damned
> death:° let Gallowes gape for Dogge, let Man goe free,°
> and let not Hempe his Wind-pipe suffocate:° but Exeter
> hath given the doome of death,° for Pax of little price.°
>
> Therefore goe speake,° the Duke will heare thy voyce;°
> and let not Bardolphs vitall thred bee cut° with edge of
> Penny-Cord, and vile reproach.°
>   Speake Captaine for
> his Life, and I will thee require.°
>   (*Henry V*, These Scripts, 2.1.450–459)

Read the speech utilising the ° to mark the end of a line, and the reader is exploring what the modern texts suggest should be the structure. Read the lines ignoring the ° and the reader is exploring what the F1 text really is. Thus both F1 and modern/Q versions can be read within the body of the text.

THE VERTICAL LINE TO THE LEFT OF THE TEXT

This will be used to mark a passage where modern editors have altered F1's verse to prose or vice versa. Here is a passage in a predominantly prose scene from *Henry V*. Modern texts and F1 agree that Williams and Fluellen should be set in prose. However, the F1 setting for Henry could be in verse, though most modern texts set it in prose too. The thin vertical line to the left of the text is a quick reminder to the reader of disagreement between Ff and modern texts (the F1 setting will always be shown, and the disputed section will be footnoted accordingly).

> King Henry Twas I indeed thou promised'st to strike,
> And thou hast given me most bitter termes.
>
> Fluellen And please your Majestie, let his Neck answere
> for it, if there is any Marshall Law in the World.
>
> King Henry How canst thou make me satisfaction?
>
> Williams All offences, my Lord, come from the heart: ne-
> ver came any from mine, that might offend your Ma-
> jestie. (*Henry V,* These Scripts, 4.1.240–247)

THE SYMBOL } SET TO THE RIGHT OF TEXT, CONNECTING TWO SPEECHES

This will be used to remind readers of the presence of what most modern texts consider to be split or shared lines, and that therefore the second speech could springboard quickly off the first, thus increasing the speed of the dialogue and debate; for example:

> Angelo Did I not tell thee yea? hadst thou not order?
> Why do'st thou aske againe?
> }
> Provost Lest I might be too rash:
> Under your good correction, I have seene
> When after execution . . .

Since there is no definitive way of determining whether Shakespeare wished the two short lines to be used as a shared or split line, or used as two separate short lines, the reader would do well to explore the moment twice. The first time the second speech could be 'springboarded' off the first as if it were a definite shared line; the second time round a tiny break could be inserted before speaking the second speech, as if a hesitation were deliberately intended. This way both possibilities of the text can be examined.

THE SYMBOL → TO THE RIGHT OF THE TEXT, JOINING TWO SHORT LINES SPOKEN BY A SINGLE CHARACTER

This indicates that though Ff has set two short lines for a single character, perhaps hinting at a minute break between the two thoughts, most modern texts have set the two short lines as one longer one. Thus the first two lines of Juliet's

> How cam'st thou hither. →

> Tell me, and wherefore?
> The Orchard walls are high, and hard to climbe

can be explored as one complete line (the interpretation of most modern texts), or, as F1 suggests, as two separate thoughts with a tiny hesitation between them. In most cases these lines will be footnoted, and possible reasons for the F1 interpretation explored.

THE OCCASIONAL USE OF THE †

This marks where F1 has been forced, in a crowded line, to set the end of the line immediately above or below the first line, flush to the right hand column. These texts will set the original as one complete line—the only instance where these scripts do not faithfully reproduce F1's line structure.

THE OCCASIONAL USE OF THE † TOGETHER WITH A FOOTNOTE (ALSO SEE P. XXXVII)

This marks where a presumed F1 compositorial mistake has led to a meaningless word being set (for example 'speeh' instead of 'speech') and, since there is a 'correct' form of the word offered by either F2–4 or Qq, the correct form of the word rather than the F1 error has been set. The footnote directs the reader to the original F1 setting reproduced at the bottom of the page.

PATTERNED BRACKETS { } SURROUNDING A PREFIX OR PART OF A STAGE DIRECTION

These will be used on the infrequent occasions where a minor alteration or addition has been made to the original F1 setting.

THE VARIED USE OF THE * AND ∞

This will change from text to text. Sometimes (as in *Hamlet*) an * will be used to show where, because of the 1606 Acte To Restraine The Abuses of Players, F1 had to alter Qq's 'God' to 'Heaven'. In other plays it may be used to show the substitution of the archaic 'a' for 'he' while in others the * and /or the ∞ may be used to denote a line from Qq or F2–4 which F1 omits.

THE SYMBOL •

This is a reminder that a character with several prefixes has returned to one previously used in the play.

THE VISUAL SYMBOLS HIGHLIGHTING KEY ITEMS WITHIN THE FIRST FOLIO

THE DROPPING OF THE TEXT A SINGLE LINE

This indicates where one sentence ends, and a new one begins (see pp. xvii–xviii).

THE BOLDING OF PUNCTUATION

This indicates the presence of the major punctuation (see pp. xviii–xxi).

UNBRACKETED STAGE DIRECTIONS

These are the ones presumed to come from the manuscript copy closest to Shakespeare's own hand (F1 sets them centred, on a separate line). They usually have a direct effect on the scene, altering what has been taking place immediately prior to its setting (see p. ix).

BRACKETED STAGE DIRECTIONS

These are the ones presumed to have been added by the Playhouse. (F1 sets them alongside the dialogue, flush to the right of the column.) They usually support, rather than alter, the onstage action (see p. ix).

(The visual difference in the two sets of directions can quickly point the reader to an unexpected aspect of an entry or exit. Occasionally an entry is set alongside the text, rather than on a separate line. This might suggest the character enters not wishing to draw attention to itself, for example, towards the end of *Macbeth,* the servant entering with the dreadful news of the moving Byrnane Wood. Again, F1 occasionally sets an exit on a separate line, perhaps stopping the onstage action altogether, as with the triumphal exit to a 'Gossips feast' at the end of *The Comedy of Errors* made by most of the reunited and/or business pacified characters, leaving the servant Dromio twins onstage to finish off the play. A footnote will be added when these unusual variations in F1's directions occur.)

As with all current texts, the final period of any bracketed or unbracketed stage direction will not be set.

ACT, SCENE, AND LINE NUMBERING SPECIFIC TO THIS TEXT

Each of these scripts will show the act and scene division from F1. They will also indicate modern act and scene division, which often differs from Ff/Qq. Modern texts suggest that in many plays full scene division was not attempted until the eighteenth century, and act division in the early texts was sometimes haphazard at best. Thus many modern texts place the act division at a point other than that set in Ff/Qq, and nearly always break Ff/Qq text up into extra scenes. When modern texts add an act or scene division which is not shared by F1, the addition will be shown in brackets within the body of each individual play as it occurs. When Ff set a new Act or scene, for clarity these texts will start a fresh page, even though this is not Ff/Qq practice

ON THE LEFT HAND SIDE OF EACH PAGE

Down the left of each page, line numbers are shown in increments of five. These refer to the lines in this text only. Where F1 prints a line containing two sentences, since these scripts set two separate lines, each line will be numbered independently.

On The Top Right Of Each Page

These numbers represent the first and last lines set on the page, and so summarise the information set down the left hand side of the text.

At The Bottom Right Of Each Page: using these scripts with other texts

At times a reader may want to compare these texts with either the original First Folio, or a reputable modern text, or both. Specially devised line numbers will make this a fairly easy proposition. These new reference numbers will be found at the bottom right of the page, just above the footnote section.

The information before the colon allows the reader to compare these texts against any photographic reproduction of the First Folio. The information after the colon allows the reader to compare these texts with a modern text, specifically the excellent *Riverside Shakespeare.*[7]

Before the colon: any photostat of the First Folio

A capital letter plus a set of numbers will be shown followed by a lowercase letter. The numbers refer the reader to a particular page within the First Folio; the capital letter before the numbers specifies whether the reader should be looking at the right hand column (R) or left hand column (L) on that particular page; the lower case letter after the numbers indicates which compositor (mainly 'a' through 'e') set that particular column. An occasional asterisk alongside the reference tells the reader that though this is the page number as set in F1, it is in fact numbered out of sequence, and care is needed to ensure, say in *Cymbeline,* the appropriate one of two 'p. 389s' is being consulted.

Since the First Folio was printed in three separate sections (the first containing the Comedies, the second the Histories, and the third the Tragedies),[8] the pages and section in which each of these scripts is to be found will be mentioned in the introduction accompanying each play. The page number refers to that printed at the top of the reproduced Folio page, and not to the number that appears at the bottom of the page of the book which contains the reproduction.

Thus, from this series of texts, page one of *Measure for Measure* shows the ref-

---

[7] Gwynne Blakemore Evans, Harry Levin, Anne Barton, Herschel Baker, Frank Kermode, Hallet D. Smith, and Marie Edel, eds., *The Riverside Shakespeare* (Copyright © 1974 by Houghton Mifflin Company). This work is chosen for its exemplary scholarship, editing principles, and footnotes.

[8] The plays known as Romances were not printed as a separate section: *Cymbeline* was set with the Tragedies, *The Winter's Tale* and *The Tempest* were set within the Comedies, and though *Pericles* had been set in Q it did not appear in the compendium until F3. *Troilus and Cressida* was not assigned to any section, but was inserted between the Histories and the Tragedies with only 2 of its 28 pages numbered.

erence 'L61–c'. This tells the reader that the text was set by compositor 'c' and can be checked against the left hand column of p. 61 of the First Folio (*Measure For Measure* being set in the Comedy Section of F1).

Occasionally the first part of the reference seen at the bottom of the page will also be seen within the text, somewhere on the right hand side of the page. This shows the reader exactly where this column has ended and the new one begins.

(As any photostat of the First Folio clearly shows, there are often sixty-five lines or more per column, sometimes crowded very close together. The late Professor Charlton Hinman employed a brilliantly simple line-numbering system (known as TLN, short for Through Line Numbering System) whereby readers could quickly be directed to any particular line within any column on any page.

The current holders of the rights to the TLN withheld permission for the system to be used in conjunction with this series of Folio Texts.)

After the colon: *The Riverside Shakespeare*

Numbers will be printed indicating the act, scene, and line numbers in *The Riverside Shakespeare*, which contain the information set on the particular page of this script. Again, using the first page of *Measure For Measure*, the reference 1.1.1–21 on page one of these scripts directs the reader to Act One Scene 1 of *The Riverside Shakespeare*; line one in *The Riverside Shakespeare* matches the first line in this text, while the last line of dialogue on page one of this text is to be found in line twenty-one of the *Riverside* version of the play.

COMMON TYPESETTING PECULIARITIES
OF THE FOLIO AND QUARTO TEXTS
(And How These Texts Present Them)

There are a few (to modern eyes) unusual contemporary Elizabethan and early Jacobean printing practices which will be retained in these scripts.

THE ABBREVIATIONS, 'S.', 'L.', 'D.', 'M.'

Ff and Qq use standard printing abbreviations when there is not enough space on a single line to fit in all the words. The most recognisable to modern eyes includes 'S.' for Saint; 'L.' for Lord; 'M.' for Mister (though this can also be short for 'Master', 'Monsieur', and on occasions even 'Mistress'); and 'D.' for Duke. These scripts will set F1 and footnote accordingly.

'Ÿ', 'W', AND ACCENTED FINAL VOWELS

Ff/Qq's two most commonly used abbreviations are not current today, viz.:
    ÿ, which is usually shorthand for either 'you'; 'thee'; 'thou'; 'thy'; 'thine'; or 'yours'
    w, usually with a ¨ above, shorthand for either 'which'; 'what'; 'when'; or 'where'.
Also, in other cases of line overcrowding, the last letter of a relatively unimportant word is omitted, and an accent placed over the preceding vowel as a marker, e.g. 'thä' for 'than'. For all such abbreviations these scripts will set F1 and footnote accordingly.

THE SPECIAL CASE OF THE QUESTION AND EXCLAMATION MARKS ('?' AND '!')

Usage

Elizabethan use of these marks differs somewhat from modern practice. Ff/Qq rarely set an exclamation mark: instead the question mark was used either both as a question mark and as an exclamation point. Thus occasionally the question mark suggests some minor emphasis in the reading.

Sentence Count

When either mark occurs in the middle of a speech, it can be followed by a capitalised or a lowercase word. When the word is lowercase (not capitalised) the sentence continues on without a break. The opposite is not always true: just because the following word is capitalised does not automatically signify the start of a new sentence, though more often than not it does.

Elizabethan rhetorical writing style allowed for words to be capitalised within a sentence, a practice continued by the F1 compositors. Several times in *The Winters Tale,* highly emotional speeches are set full of question marks followed by capitalised words. Each speech could be either one long sentence of ongoing passionate rush, or up to seven shorter sentences attempting to establish self-control.

The final choice belongs to the individual reader, and in cases where such alternatives arise, the passages will be boxed, footnoted, and the various possibilities discussed.

THE ENDING OF SPEECHES WITH NO PUNCTUATION, OR PUNCTUATION OTHER THAN A PERIOD

Quite often F1–2 will not show punctuation at the end of a speech, or sometimes set a colon (:) or a comma (,) instead. Some commentators suggest the setting of anything other than a period was due to compositor carelessness, and that omission occurred either for the same reason, or because the text was so full it came flush to the right hand side of the column and there was no room left for the final punctuation to be set. Thus modern texts nearly always end a speech with the standard period (.), question mark (?), or exclamation mark (!), no matter what F1–2 have set.

However, omission doesn't always occur when a line is full, and F2, though making over sixteen hundred unauthorised typographical corrections of F1 (more than eight hundred of which are accepted by most modern texts), rarely replaces an offending comma or colon with a period, or adds missing periods—F3 is the first to make such alterations on a large scale basis. A few commentators, while acknowledging some of the omissions/mistakes are likely to be due to compositor or scribal error, suggest that ending the speech with anything other than a period (or not ending the speech at all) might indicate that the character with the speech immediately following is in fact interrupting this first speaker.

These texts will set F1, footnote accordingly, and sometimes discuss the possible effect of the missing or 'incorrect' punctuation.

THE SUBSTITUTIONS OF 'i/I' FOR 'j/J' AND 'u' FOR 'v'

In both Ff/Qq words now spelled as 'Jove' or 'Joan' are often set as 'Iove' or 'Ioan'. To avoid confusion, these texts will set the modern version of the word. Similarly, words with 'v' in the middle are often set by Ff/Qq with a 'u'; thus the modern word 'avoid' becomes 'auoid'. Again, these texts will set the modern version of the word, without footnote acknowledgement.

ALTERNATIVE SETTINGS OF A WORD WHERE DIFFERENT SPELLINGS MAINTAIN THE SAME MEANING

Ff/Qq occasionally set, what appears to modern eyes, an archaic spelling of a word for which there is a more common modern alternative, for example 'murther' for murder, 'burthen' for burden, 'moe' for more, 'vilde' for vile. Some modern texts set the Ff/Qq spelling, some modernise. These texts will set the F1 spelling throughout.

ALTERNATIVE SETTINGS OF A WORD WHERE DIFFERENT SPELLINGS SUGGEST DIFFERENT MEANINGS

Far more complicated is the situation where, while an Elizabethan could substitute one word formation for another and still imply the same thing, to modern eyes the substituted word has a entirely different meaning to the one it has replaced. The following is by no means an exclusive list of the more common dual-spelling, dual-meaning words:

anticke–antique	mad–made	sprite–spirit
born–borne	metal–mettle	sun–sonne
hart–heart	mote–moth	travel–travaill
human–humane	pour–(powre)–power	through–thorough
lest–least	reverent–reverend	troth–truth
lose–loose	right–rite	whether–whither

Some of these doubles offer a metrical problem too; for example 'sprite', a one syllable word, versus 'spirit'. A potential problem occurs in *A Midsummer Nights Dream*, where provided the modern texts set Q1's 'thorough', the scansion pattern of elegant magic can be established, whereas F1's more plebeian 'through' sets up a much more awkward and clumsy moment.

These texts will set the F1 reading, and footnote where the modern texts' substitution of a different word formation has the potential to alter the meaning (and sometimes scansion) of the line.

'THEN' AND 'THAN'

These two words, though their neutral vowels sound different to modern ears, were almost identical to Elizabethan speakers and readers, despite their different meanings. Ff and Qq make little distinction between them, setting them interchangeably. In these scripts the original printings will be used, and the modern reader should soon get used to substituting one for the other as necessary.

'I', AND 'AY'

Ff/Qq often print the personal pronoun 'I' and the word of agreement 'aye' simply as 'I'. Again, the modern reader should quickly get used to this and make the substitution whenever necessary. The reader should also be aware that very occasionally either word could be used and the phrase make perfect sense, even though different meanings would be implied.

'MY SELFE/HIM SELFE/HER SELFE' VERSUS 'MYSELF /HIMSELF / HERSELF'

Generally Ff/Qq separate the two parts of the word, 'my selfe' while most modern texts set the single word 'myself'. The difference is vital, based on Elizabethan philosophy. Elizabethans regarded themselves as composed of two parts, the corporeal 'I', and the more spiritual part, the 'selfe'. Thus when an Elizabethan character refers to 'my selfe', he or she is often referring to what is to all intents and purposes a separate being, even if that being is a particular part of him- or herself. Thus soliloquies can be thought of as a debate between the 'I' and 'my selfe', and in such speeches, even though there may be only one character onstage, it's as if there were two distinct entities present.

These texts will show F1 as set.

FOOTNOTE CODE
(shown in two forms, the first alphabetical, the second grouping the codes by topic)

To help the reader focus on a particular topic or research aspect, a special code has been developed for these texts. Each footnote within the footnote section at the bottom of each page of text has a single letter or series of letters placed in front of it guiding readers to one specific topic; thus 'SPD' will direct readers to footnotes just dealing with songs, poems, and doggerel.

ALPHABETICAL FOOTNOTE CODING

A	asides
AB	abbreviation
ADD	a passage modern texts have added to their texts from F2–4/Qq
ALT	a passage (including act and scene division) that has been altered by modern texts without any Ff/Qq authority
COMP	a setting probably influenced by compositor interference
F	concerning disputed facts within the play
FL	foreign language
L	letter or letters
LS	alterations in line structure
M	Shakespeare's use of the scansion of magic (trochaic and seven syllables)
N	a name modern texts have changed or corrected for easier recognition
O	F1 words or phrases substituted for a Qq oath or blasphemy
OM	passage, line, or word modern texts omit or suggest omitting
P	change in prefix assigned to a character
PCT	alterations to F1's punctuation by modern and/or contemporary texts
Q	material rejected or markedly altered by Qq not usually set by modern texts
QO	oaths or blasphemies set in Qq not usually set by modern texts
SD	stage directions added or altered by modern texts
SP	a solo split line for a single character (see pp. xv–xvi above)

SPD	matters concerning songs, poems, or doggerel
?ST	where, because of question marks within the passage, the final choice as to the number of sentences is left to the reader's discretion
STRUCT	a deliberate change from the F1 setting by these texts
UE	an unusual entrance (set to the side of the text) or exit (set on a separate line)
VP	F1's verse altered to prose or vice versa, or lines indistinguishable as either
W	F1's word or phrase altered by modern texts
WHO	(in a convoluted passage) who is speaking to whom
WS	F1 line structure altered because of casting off problems (see pp. x–xi above)

FOOTNOTE CODING BY TOPIC

STAGE DIRECTIONS, ETC.

A	asides
P	change in prefix assigned to a character
SD	stage directions added or altered by modern texts
UE	an unusual entrance (set to the side of the text) or exit (set on a separate line)
WHO	(in a convoluted passage) who is speaking to whom

LINE STRUCTURE AND PUNCTUATION, ETC.

L	letter or letters
LS	alterations in line structure
M	Shakespeare's use of the scansion of magic (trochaic and seven syllables)
PCT	alterations to F1's punctuation by modern and/or contemporary texts
SPD	matters concerning songs, poems, or doggerel
?ST	where, because of question marks within the passage, the final choice as to the number of sentences is left to the reader's discretion
SP	a solo split line for a single character (see pp. xv–xvi above)
VP	F1's verse altered to prose or vice versa, or lines indistinguishable as either

WS   F1 line structure altered because of casting off problems (see pp. x–xi above)

CHANGES TO WORDS AND PHRASES

AB   abbreviation

F   concerning disputed facts within the play

FL   foreign language

N   a name modern texts have changed or corrected for easier recognition

O   F1 words or phrases substituted for a Qq oath or blasphemy

QO   oaths or blasphemies set in Qq not usually set by modern texts

W   F1's word or phrase altered by modern texts

CHANGES ON A LARGER SCALE AND OTHER UNAUTHORISED CHANGES

ADD   a passage modern texts have added to their texts from F2–4/Qq

ALT   a passage (including act and scene division) that has been altered by modern texts without any Ff/Qq authority

COMP   a setting probably influenced by compositor interference

OM   passage, line, or word modern texts omit or suggest omitting

Q   material rejected or markedly altered by Qq not usually set by modern texts

STRUCT a deliberate change from the F1 setting by these texts

ONE MODERN CHANGE FREQUENTLY NOTED IN THESE TEXTS

'MINUTE' CHANGES TO THE SYLLABLE LENGTH OF FF LINES

As noted above on pages xi–xii, modern texts frequently correct what commentators consider to be large scale metric deficiencies, often to the detriment of character and scene. There are many smaller changes made too, especially when lines are either longer or shorter than the norm of pentameter by 'only' one or two syllables. These changes are equally troublesome, for there is a highly practical theatrical rule of thumb guideline to such irregularities, viz.:

if lines are slightly **longer** than pentameter, then the characters so involved have too much information coursing through them to be contained within the 'norms' of proper verse, occasionally even to the point of losing self-control

if lines are slightly **shorter** than ten syllables, then either the information therein contained or the surrounding action is creating a momentary (almost need to breath) hesitation, sometimes suggesting a struggle to maintain self-control

These texts will note all such alterations, usually offering the different syllable counts per line as set both by F1 and by the altered modern texts, often with a brief suggestion as to how the original structural 'irregularity' might reflect onstage action.

FINALLY, A BRIEF WORD ABOUT THE COMPOSITORS [9]

Concentrated research into the number of the compositors and their habits began in the 1950s and, for a while, it was thought five men set the First Folio, each assigned a letter, 'A' through 'E'.

'E' was known to be a seventeen-year-old apprentice whose occasional mishaps both in copying text and securing the type to the frame have led to more than a few dreadful lapses, notably in *Romeo and Juliet*, low in the left column on p. 76 of the Tragedies, where in sixteen F1 lines he commits seven purely typographical mistakes. Compositor 'B' set approximately half of F1, and has been accused of being cavalier both with copying text and not setting line ending punctuation when the line is flush to the column edge. He has also been accused of setting most of the so called 'solo' split lines, though a comparison of other compositors' habits suggests they did so too, especially the conglomerate once considered to be the work of a single compositor known as 'A'. It is now acknowledged that the work set by 'A' is probably the work of at least two and more likely five different men, bringing the total number of compositors having worked on F1 to nine ('A' times five, and 'B' through 'E').

It's important to recognise that the work of these men was sometimes flawed. Thus the footnotes in these texts will point the reader to as many examples as possible which current scholarship and research suggest are in error. These errors fall into two basic categories. The first is indisputable, that of pure typographical mistakes ('wh?ch' for 'which'): the second, frequently open to challenge, is failure to copy exactly the text (Qq or manuscript) which F1 has used as its source material.

As for the first, these texts place the symbol † before a footnote marker within the text (not in the footnote section), a combination used only to point to a purely typographical mistake. Thus in the error-riddled section of *Romeo and Juliet* quoted above, p. 109 of this script shows fourteen footnote markers, seven of them coupled with the symbol †. Singling out these typographical-only markers alerts the reader to compositor error, and that (usually) the 'correct' word or phrase has been set within the text. Thus the reader doesn't have to bother with the footnote below unless they have a morbid curiosity to find out what the error actually is. Also, by definition, the more † appearing in a passage, the worse set that passage is.

As to the second series of (sometimes challengeable) errors labelled poor copy work, the footnotes will alert the reader to the alternative Qq word or phrase usage preferred by most modern texts, often discussing the alternatives in detail, especially when there seems to be validity to the F1 setting.

---

[9]   Readers are directed to the ground breaking work of Alice Walker, and also to the ongoing researches of Paul Werstine and Peter W. M. Blayney.

Given the fluid state of current research, more discoveries are bound to be published as to which compositor set which F1 column long after these texts go to print. Thus the current assignation of compositors at the bottom of each of these scripts' pages represents what is known at this moment, and will be open to reassessment as time goes by.

A CAVEAT: THE COMPOSITORS AND 'SINGLE SPLIT LINES' (SEE PP. XV–XVI)

Many commentators suggest single split lines are not Shakespearean dramatic necessity, but compositorial invention to get out of a typesetting dilemma. Their argument is threefold:

first, as mentioned on pp. x–xi, because of 'white space' a small amount of text would have to be artificially expanded to fill a large volume of what would otherwise be empty space: therefore, even though the column width could easily accommodate regular verse lines, the line or lines would be split in two to fill an otherwise embarrassing gap

second, even though the source documents the compositors were using to set F1 showed material as a single line of verse, occasionally there was too much text for the F1 column to contain it as that one single line: hence the line had to be split in two

third, the device was essentially used by compositor B.

There is no doubt that sometimes single split lines did occur for typesetting reasons, but it should be noted that:

single split lines are frequently set well away from white space problems

often the 'too-much-text-for-the-F1-column-width' problem is solved by setting the last one or two words of the overly lengthy line either as a new line, or as an overflow or underflow just above the end of the existing line without resorting to the single split line

all compositors seem to employ the device, especially the conglomerate known as 'A' and compositor E.

As regards the following text, while at times readers will be alerted to the fact that typographical problems could have had an influence on the F1 setting, when single split lines occur their dramatic potential will be discussed, and readers are invited to explore and accept or reject the setting accordingly.

INTRODUCTION TO THE TEXT OF
THE FIRST PART OF HENRY THE FOURTH
with the Life and Death of HENRY Sirnamed HOT-SPURRE [1]
pages 46 - 73 of the History Section [2]
All Act, Scene, and line numbers will refer to the
Applause text below unless otherwise stated.

Current research places the play as number fifteen in the canon. It was set in tandem with *The life and death of King Richard the Second.*

Since the play thematically follows *The life and death of Richard II*, precedes *The Merry Wives of Windsor* (finished by Spring 1597) and was published in 1598, commentators are agreed the play dates from late 1596 - early 1597.

SCHOLARS' ASSESSMENT

Scholars offer any would-be editor a vast array of contemporary documents to be assessed - one fragment of a Quarto, six full Quartos, foul papers,[3] two different transcripts, a prompt book and a First Folio. [4] Beginning with Shakespeare's foul papers, two different trails developed: the first was

- Quarto 0 (Q0) of 1598, probably taken from a scribal copy of the foul papers (not the papers themselves as once thought), of which only one printing house sheet remains.
- Quarto 1 (Q1) also of 1598, essentially a speedy (see the heading 'Oldcastle' below) and accurate reprint of Q0 [5] and thus also based on the foul papers, which was followed by
- Quarto 2 (Q2) of 1599, Quarto 3 (Q3) of 1604, Quarto 4 (Q4) of 1608, Quarto 5 (Q5) of 1613, Quarto 6 (Q6) of 1622, all essentially derivative of the one it followed.

However, to establish the First Folio (F1) of 1623 one must return to the foul papers and follow the second trail: from the foul papers and, independent of the first scribal copy, came a prompt book, the prompt book begat a literary transcript, the literary transcript was used in combination with Q6, and thus F1 was born.

---

[1] For a detailed examination, see Wells, Stanley and Taylor, Gary (eds.). *William Shakespeare: A Textual Companion.* Oxford: Clarendon Press. 1987. pages 329 - 339: for a detailed analysis of the play's contents, see any of the Recommended Modern Texts.

[2] *Mr. William Shakespeare's Comedies, Histories, & Tragedies*, 1623.

[3] 'Foul papers' refers to Shakespeare's first draft, with all the original crossings out and blots intact: a prompt-book has been prepared by the Playhouse (copied from either fair or foul papers) with detailed information added necessary for staging a theatrical performance.

[4] An excellent examination of the texts, the scribal copy of Q0 and the various reworkings thereafter can be found in *A Textual Companion*, pages 329 - 332.

[5] *A Textual Companion* suggests Q1 was in fact set from the 'same font' as Q0 (page 329).

The consensus as to authority is best expressed by *The Arden Shakespeare King Henry IV Part 1*, see Recommended Texts at the end of this introduction, which lists in full the major changes between the various Qq's and Q1/F , pages lxxix - lxxv.

> 'The conclusion . . . [is] . . . that Qq0,1, are the only substantive sources, that the prompt-book played no discernible part, and that the variants in later Qq and F have authority no greater than that of later editions . . .' (page lxxv).

Significant later Q/F1 variations from Q1 include eradicating obvious profanity, though as with *Hamlet*, the excision of all profanity was not as complete as in other plays; anti-sophistications (i.e. setting 'he's' for the more literary 'he is'); adding Act and Scene division; and tidying of prefixes. Consequently *A Textual Companion* rejects over 250 F1 variants, and lists fifty Q passages involving nearly one hundred and twenty lines that needed to be altered for *The Oxford Shakespeares.* [6]

• **HOW THIS TEXT WILL DEAL WITH OATHS AND SOPHISTICATIONS**

In pointing to evidence of F1 smoothing out some of the more rough edged phrases and abbreviations set in Q, commentators often rather crassly dismiss the F1 wording as 'what the actors should (and will) say' (the opening of Act Two Scene 1 with the Carriers, Ostler and Gads-hill often being singled out as example, pages 23 - 5 this text). And as with several of the History plays, there are far more oaths in Q and modern texts than the 1606 Acte to restraine the Abuses of Players [7] allowed F1 to maintain - with most modern texts adding 50 or more to the play. Thus while many differences between most modern texts and F1 have to be accounted for, readers shouldn't have to pick their way through too many footnotes.

Thus this text will take two approaches. The more unusual sophistications/anti-sophistications will be footnoted as and when they occur. In addition, at least fifty more are common throughout many of the plays where quarto and Folio versions both exist ('mine' for 'my', 'a' for 'he', etc.), and to list each of these will add far more notes than are worthwhile. Thus these words will have an asterisk (*) set in front, and reader should have little or no difficulty in realising what the modern Qq based variation might be.

The * will also be applied on the plus twenty occasions F1 substitutes the inoffensive 'heaven' for Qq's more forceful 'God'. As with elisions/sophistications, when F1 removes a full Qq oath the text will be footnoted accordingly.

---

[6] Wells, Stanley and Taylor, Gary (eds.). *The Oxford Shakespeare, William Shakespeare, The Complete Works, Original Spelling Edition/Modern Spelling Edition.* Oxford: The Clarendon Press. 1986

[7] An Act of Parliament to prevent any unnecessary blasphemy, oaths, or questionable religious references from being printed. Any pre-1606 material being printed had to excise all such references before being given a license to reprint (hence the differences between many quarto and F1 versions of the same plays).

THE OLDCASTLE-FALSTAFFE CONTROVERSY, WITH THE ROSSILL-HARVEY FALLOUT

The character now known as Falstaffe was originally named Oldcastle, which quickly got Shakespeare into a lot of political trouble. Indeed in the Epilogue to *The Second Part of Henry the Fourth* Shakespeare apologises. Referring to a future play - presumably *The Life of Henry the Fift*, in which paradoxically the Oldcastle/Falstaffe figure dies offstage without ever making an appearance - Shakespeare writes

> Fal-
> staffe shall dye of a sweat, unlesse he already be kill'd with your hard Opinions:
> For Old-Castle dyed a Martyr, and this is not the man.

The problem was that though historically there was an Oldcastle at the time of Henry IV (nowhere near the Vice figure Shakespeare portrays) his powerful descendants included members of the Cobham (Brooke) family, the 7th Lord of whom had held the post of Lord Chamberlain to Queen Elizabeth. The 8th Lord protested, and the name was hastily changed to one reminiscent of the cowardly figure already seen in *The first Part of Henry the Sixt*, Sir John Falstaffe. [8] So expeditious was the change that the frontispiece of Q1 1598, printed hard on the heels of Q0, contains the proclamation 'with the humorous conceits of Sir John Falstaffe'.

Whereas Oldcastle was an earlier historical figure named in *Holinshed*,[9] two others which might also have given offence to contemporary aristocracy were not. Rossill was a corruption of Russell, the family name of the Earl of Bedford and Harvey was the surname of the Earl of Southampton's stepfather. Thus, though still named in the dialogue (page 10, line 1. 2. 179) a presumably 'politically influenced' change was effected for the prefixes from Q1 onwards and F, with Harvey becoming Bardolfe and Rossill renamed Peto. [10]

While the Oldcastle/Falstaffe controversy does not affect the prefixes, there is the problem of which characters accompany Falstaffe throughout the play. As footnote #6 page 10, points out, though Poines refers to Harvey and Rossill being with Falstaffe, it is Bardolfe and Peto who are set both entry and dialogue (and Gads-hill via a later entry). Most modern texts correct the Q/Ff dialogue accordingly.

---

[8] Whether Shakespeare was being extra cautious in not setting the original surname used by Holinshed (for citation see next footnote), Fastolfe, is a matter of conjecture.

[9] Holinshed, Raphael. *Chronicles Of England, Scotland And Ireland*. 1587 (2nd. edition) .

[10] *The Oxford Shakespeares* are the first major texts to return to referring to the characters as Old-castle, Rossill and Harvey, though they do not carry this through for either *The Second Part of Henry the Fourth* or *The Merry Wives of Windsor*

THE TEXT

Commentators agree that B set 30 columns (misnumbering what should have been pages 47 and 48, setting 49 and 50 instead), though there is some disagreement as which compositor set the other 22. *A Textual Companion* suggests J, a claim more recently denied by Blayney in the 1996 reprint of The W. W. Norton *First Folio*,[11] who plumps for A.

Of the several Q lines omitted by F1, the most important are for Prince John, who, asked by his older brother Hal to free the captured enemy rebel Dowglas without ransom (a direct slap at his father's authority), sides publicly and whole-heartedly with Hal via the two lines (as found in Q1 - 4) [12]

> I thanke your grace for this high curtesie,
> Which I shall give away immediatly.

F1'S STAGE MANAGEMENT OF THE PLAY

PREFIXES

These present little problem, except for the variable spellings of Bardolfe within the dialogue (Bardolphe is also used here and in *The Second Part of Henry the Fourth*, but never in *The Merry Wives of Windsor*). [13]

There is the usual generic problem in that while a direction sets 'Enter Travellers' (page 30), three prefixes refer simply to 'Tra.', which could be one speaking three times, or different characters taking different lines. There are also the usual unspecified number of Musicians, Lords, Guards and 'others'.

There is an interesting dichotomy for the future Henry the Fifth. While he is referred to as Hal (or occasionally Hall) throughout the dialogue of the play, his prefix never alters from Prince, perhaps a reminder of the constancy of his personal philosophy as expressed so clearly in his first soliloquy, 'I know you all. . . ' (page 12, 1. 2. 211 and on). [14]

THE USUAL LACK OF INNER STAGE DIRECTIONS

As usual in an F1 (or Qq) play, quite a few of them are simply implied in the dialogue rather than being spelled out. This would have presented no problem to the original actors and prompt book holder, for it was second nature for them to fill in many of the smaller details without extra annotation. Thus whatever minor moments did not make their way to the various publishing houses were not added by the publishers since, as often as not, they weren't really missing if the text in question was closely followed. Thus in many of the

---

[11]   Blayney, Peter W.M. (ed.). *The Norton Facsimile (The First Folio Of Shakespeare)*. New York: W.W.Norton & Company, Inc. 1996

[12]   See footnote #3, page 119.

[13]   Poynes is also spelled as Pointz in one entry and perhaps one prefix (though more so in *Part II*)

[14]   His first stage direction refers to him as 'Henry Prince of Wales': thereafter he is referred to either as 'Prince of Wales', or simply 'Prince'.

scenes, a reader can get by without such directions simply by paying careful attention to the action of the play as the dialogue unfolds. (However, when the action remains obscure, this text, as all others in this series, will add extra information via footnotes.)

There is the usual post-event dialogue to explain an earlier need, for example Hotspurre's 'The king hath many marching in his coats.' (line 5. 2. 135, page 108) explains why Dowglas mistook (and killed) Blunt for King Henry, Blunt being dressed as one of Henry's several decoys.

There is the usual pre-event dialogue which eradicates the need for any further directions, such as Bardolfe's 'on with your Vizards' (line 2, 2, 61, page 29) to get all the would-be thieves, royal and commoner alike, masked.

Directions for the various fights are usually full and complete, however other stage directions are not always at their best. Thus not even Hal's explanation can fully establish the ins-and-outs as he and Poynes tease Francis (pages 38 - 40). Similarly, Falstaffe's physical demonstrations as he fibs about the supposed fight (with an ever increasing number of opponents - at the last tally 50!) in explanation as to how the money he stole was in turn stolen from him (pages 43 - 5) and the details of the play-acting by Falstaffe and Hal of the forthcoming interview between Hal and his father Henry IVth (pages 51 - 4) are left to the reader's imagination.

ENTRIES AND EXITS

In like fashion, these are not always complete.

No exit is given for Worcester after the King's blunt dismissal 'get thee gone' (page 13, line 1. 3. 15): it is only a side set (re-)entry more than one hundred lines later (page 17) that suggests he obeyed (see Unusual Entries And Exits below).

Sometimes, those needed in the scene are not always brought in with the principal character. Thus 'Enter Falstaffe' (page 41 - following the failed robbery) neglects to add that Gads-hill, Bardolfe and Peto accompany him - that fact only comes up some ninety lines later when Gads-hill starts talking about the supposed fight whereby they lost the money, and when Hal addresses the other two by name more than 90 lines after that. Also, Dowglas should be included in page 105, pre line 5. 2. 30 'Enter Hotspurre', since there is a direction for his exit just seven lines later.

Sometimes a direction is just too vague. Page 28's 'They Whistle' hardly explains that Hal, Poynes and Peto come forward to join Falstaffe, having led him to believe they have abandoned him well away from his horse, in the dark, in unfamiliar countryside.

• **WORCESTER'S UNUSUAL ENTRY AND EXIT**

As to special entries and exits, there is an excellent side-set (self-effacing) entry for Worcester (page 17). Most F1 entries are set centered on a line separate from the surrounding dialogue. This entry is set as an exit (to the right of the text, on the same line as the dialogue that precedes it), and since crammed space does not account for the setting it is possible that it might signify either the entering character does not wish to draw attention to itself or where the reaction of those on-stage is equally important as the entry itself. Here the former is more likely, since Worcester was previously kicked out by the King. The setting of the entry suggests he sneaks back in (knowing the King departed five lines earlier) hoping to be unseen except by his own relatives Hotspurre and Northumberland.

Much later in the play, again dismissed by the King, this time as a bone fide rebel leaving unsuccessful peace negotiations, he is given the exact opposite. Most F1 exits are set to the right of the text, on the same line as the dialogue that precedes it. Here his exit is set as an entry (centered on a line separate from the surrounding dialogue), and with white space [15] not being responsible for the setting, it is possible that this particular exit (page 102) is attention-grabbing and demands that all on-stage action cease until Worcester's departure is completed.

ASIDES & WHO-TO'S [16]

These sometimes need further elaboration, for while it is reasonable to assume that the remarks about the Welsh Lady between Hotspurre and his Lady are private (pages 66 - 7), it's more than likely Hotspurre's earlier put downs of Glendower were meant to be heard (pages 58 - 60). And while it is usual to mark as asides Hal and Poynes' barbed comments as Falstaffe explains how he defeated his (imaginary) combatants, there may be much mileage for some or all of them to be said loud enough for all, including Falstaffe, to hear (page 45).

MODERN INTERVENTIONS

Unlike *Macbeth* with its swath of large-scale textual changes, most of the alterations in this play are of the 'nip and tuck' variety. Even so, the enforced rationalisation they bring to characters who are not always rational or in self-control can do a great amount of unnecessary theatrical reworking.

---

[15] The term used to describe the condition of a page with so little dialogue that there are large sections of empty space surrounding the text, leading modern commentators to suggest the compositors often restructured the original line sequence to create more lines than were first set so as to occupy some of the blank space which would otherwise lie empty.

[16] Asides are lines spoken by one character either directly to the audience, or to a small sub-group within a larger group on-stage, and not meant to be heard by anyone else. 'Who-to's' are suggestions as to which particular on-stage character out of a larger-group is being addressed by a particular remark. Both are usually modern text additions, for Q/F rarely set such indications.

IRREGULAR LINES: (POSSIBLE) CRACKS UNDERLYING PUBLIC STATEMENTS

Prior to the line structure alterations occasioned by many modern texts, readers could discover cracks in the private nature of individuals as the underlying tension comes pouring through via F1's (often supported by Q) irregular settings.

It's useful to remember irregular lines do not dictate how a character should speak, but simply suggest that the character cannot speak pure poetry at that particular moment. The irregularities are not 'hopelessly corrupt' but occur where the reader would not expect the character(s) to be capable of speaking rationally or 'normally' or 'poetically' because of the inordinate strain they are undergoing. As such, great theatrical attention ought to be paid to them. (The short, less than ten syllable lines do not suggest that the character must pause for the full value of the 'silent' or missing syllables - they merely indicate that the character is incapable of finishing a line. Similarly, the long lines do not suggest the character should gabble or yell so as to get all the syllables into what would be a ten syllable line, just that the moment they are undergoing is so complex emotionally and/or intellectually that it cannot be fitted within the confines of a normal poetic line.)

For example, late in the play the situation is beginning to look desperate for Hotspurre's and his ally Dowglas' rebellion. Northumberland, Hotspurre's father, has used an unspecified illness, dismissed later in *The Second Part of Henry the Fourth* as 'crafty-sick', as the excuse both for not joining his son in battle and for failing to send much needed troops.

Dowglas attempts to rally enthusiasm, via some very irregular Qq/F1 lines. Starting with a shared split line, he offers the optimistic

> Faith and so wee should,
> Where now remaines a sweet reversion.   (9 - 10)
> We may boldly spend, upon the hope   (9)
> Of what is to come in: (6)
> A comfort of retyrement lives in this.   (10)
> > (page 85, lines 4. 1. 61 - 5)

The gaps and hesitations suggest little or no response, and that Dowglas has to work hard to establish his argument. Most modern texts revamp the text to the much more regular

> Faith and so wee should, where now remaines   (9)
> A sweet reversion. We may boldly spend,   (10-11)
> Upon the hope of what is to come in: (10)

Similar cracks are to be found in Hotspurre's admiring welcome of the king's friend and envoy Sir Walter Blunt (page 93, lines 4. 3. 38 - 9), and in the King's decision to hold a 'Councell' meeting at Windsor (page 4, lines 1. 1. 112 - 3). But perhaps the most peculiar resetting affects Westmerland's having to inform the King of Hotspurre's wonderful military conquest against the 'Scot' Dowglas, knowing it will depress the King even further when comparing the public reputation of Hotspurre to that of his son Hal. Qq/F1 set three lines of tiny hesitations, whereas some modern texts jam the passage together to create a monstrous first line of between thirteen and fifteen syllables. The modern texts'

> That ever-valiant and approoved Scot, at Holmedon met   (13-15)
> Where they did spend a sad and bloody houre: (10)

is a far cry from Qq/F1's

> That ever-valiant and approoved Scot,   (9-11)
> At Holmedon met, where they did spend   (8)
> A sad and bloody houre: (6)
>
> (page 2, lines 1. 1. 57 - 9)

Since the modern resetting is, in its own entirely different way, as irregular as the passage it sought to replace, why bother?

F1'S SINGLE SPLIT LINES [17] SUGGEST UNDERLYING TENSION

This certainly could be the case for Hotspurre's response to Vernon's news of the King's arrival with 'strong and mightie preparation'. The gap offered by F1's

> He shall be welcome too.   (6)
> Where is his Sonne,   (4)
> The nimble-footed Mad-Cap, Prince of Wales
>
> (page 87, lines 4. 1. 106 - 8)

allows a momentary silence which almost denies Hotspurre's spoken braggadocio. Q/most modern texts set the two lines as one. Perhaps emphasising the strain of campaigning with inadequate forces are two more such settings as Hotspurre receives the news of his father's essential abandoning of him. [18]

Then there are the moments when Hotspurre deliberately tries Glendower's patience with several non too subtle put-downs, for example as Glendower boasts that at his birth

> The heavens were all on fire, the Earth did
> tremble
>
> (page 59, lines 3. 1. 25 - 9)

Hotspurre's reply is set as a single line by Q/most modern texts, though the gaps in the F1 setting

> Oh, then the Earth shooke   (5)
> To see the Heavens on fire,   (6-7)
> And not in feare of your Nativitie.

highlights the insult for speaker and shocked listeners alike.

---

[17]   These are two or more short verse lines, set for a <u>single</u> character, which if placed together would form a single full line of verse. These lines are rarely reproduced as set by any modern text : see the General Introduction, pages xv - xvi for further discussion.

[18]   See the last seven lines at the bottom of page 83, lines 4. 1. 13 - 21, though there is the possibility white space is responsible for the setting (F1 History page 65, right hand column).

(POSSIBLE) SHIFTS IN PUBLIC BEHAVIOUR INHERENT IN F1'S VERSE/PROSE COMBINATIONS

Such F1 shifts are small-scale but significant. The distinction between the two is not mere pedantry: verse implies some harmony and grace in self-expression, prose brings a more prosaic, everyday quality to the dialogue. Theatrically it is usually well worthwhile to note when such F1 shifts from prose to verse (and vice versa) occur - the transition can suggest a change in attitude in or between the speakers so involved.

The final two speech demand by Hotspurre's Lady to be told what is so disturbing her husband, the little-finger-breaking threat (page 35, lines 2. 3. 95 - 107), is set by Q/F1 as prose. And even though this marks a move from the dignity of reasoned verse argument to the more personal physical husband and wife spat, most modern texts recast it as verse, the overall style of the scene. Again, as Hal begins to face the 'Sherife' searching for Falstaffe to bring him to account for the earlier theft from the Travellers, Qq/F start the sequence in easy-going everyday prose (pages 55 - 6). As the carrier becomes more insistent Hal is shown moving into verse (pulling rank perhaps?) as he gives his word Falstaffe will render an account of himself the following day. Most modern texts do not make the verse shift at the top of page 56, line 2. 4. 576.

Nor do they set the prose-verse shift, or vice-versa, of two wonderfully teasing moments, both involving Falstaffe. As he play-acts the King, having reduced the Hostesse to tears of helpless laughter, he then mock-orders

> For Gods sake Lords, convey my trustfull Queen,
> For teares doe stop the floud-gates of her eyes.
>
> (page 51, lines 2. 4. 443 - 4)

before shifting back to prose, a joyful play-acting moment if ever there was one. The other starts with a serious request from Falstaffe, in one of his extraordinarily rare verse utterances - perhaps occasioned by the sombre verse peace negotiations just unsuccessfully concluded (page 102, lines 5. 1. 128 - 132)

> Hal, if thou see me downe in the battell,
> And bestride me, so; 'tis a point of friendship

being dismissed by Hal

> Nothing but a Colossus can do thee that frendship
> Say thy prayers, and farewell.

which in turn elicits another Falstaffe verse line

> I would it were bed time Hal, and all well.

before the scene falls back into prose

> Prince   Why, thou ows't heaven a death.
>
> Falstaffe   'Tis not due yet: I would be loath to pay him
>   before his day. What neede . . .

MODERN PUNCTUATION REDUCING F1'S 'LESS THAN-IN CONTROL' MOMENTS

Some modern changes in punctuation are very useful, such as the addition of dashes as Falstaffe undercuts his own 'modest' behaviour (see footnotes #2 - #4, page 74. But, as usual, occasional fiddling reduces emotionally driven situations, such as Falstaffe's laying retaliatory invective on Hal, as doubts are heaped on Falstaffe's less than truthful account of how he in turn was relieved of the money he stole from the Act Two Travellers. F1's ungrammatical period marked *

> Away you Starveling, you Elfe-skin, you dried
> Neats tongue, Bulles-pissell, you stocke-fish: O for breth
> to utter.* What is like to thee? You Tailors yard . . .
> (page 46, lines 2. 4. 276 - 80)

not only supports Falstaffe's claim to be out of breath, it gives him a moment to search for more insults. The Q/modern texts' setting of a comma for the asterisked period simply maintains the speech's ongoing flow.

There are also several passages where the number of sentences within a speech will determine the flow (or otherwise) of the moment. The nature of debate suggests a clear stepping stone from one idea to the next. This is normally marked in Elizabethan texts by a series of well developed sentences. As a rule of thumb, the longer the sentence, the more passionate the drive of the argument, or the free-wheeling nature of self-expression: the shorter the sentence, the clearer, more precise the issue is (while very short sentences suggest the need for exploration, debate and entertaining discussion is long past).[19]

This play presents an interesting problem not often shared by other Ff texts, one which the imagination of the reader must decide interpretation. In Elizabethan/ Jacobean orthography, (the manner of setting any matter down on paper), a question mark followed by a capital letter does not necessarily indicate the start of a new sentence. In verse, the matter is further complicated when the question mark is at the end of the line because, as a matter of post 1600 typographical convention, the new line that follows always starts with a capital letter (new sentence or no). Hence the occasional question, how many sentences are there in a particular passage? - the fewer the sentences, the more sustained the line of attack.

Thus, the opening ten lines of Hotspurre's Lady where she starts to question him (page 33, lines 2. 3. 49 - 62), could be set as anywhere between one and eight sentences, and the last eleven lines of Henry's ruthless questioning, challenging, reputation-damaging attacks on Hal (page 71, lines 3. 2. 124 - 135), could be set anywhere between one and five.[20]

---

[19] Readers are referred to Freeman, Neil: *Shakespeare's First Texts*. Vancouver: 1994

[20] Nowhere is the question more pertinent than with Falstaffe's wonderful homily on 'honour' (page 103). There are no fewer than fourteen question marks followed by a capital letter. Thus the speech could be as few as twelve spoken sentences or as long as twenty-six.

QUICKNESS AND INTERRUPTION OF CONVERSATION RATHER THAN DEBATE

Extended passages of shared split lines are few, Spevack [21] finding just 46, not many for such a long play. Thus it would seem that most characters prefer to make speeches on firm-set opinions rather than really debate with an option for change.[22]

The few such shared lines do serve a useful purpose when they occur, as with Vernon's jumping in on Hotspurre's wish for news of Glendower, and Hotspurre's response to the size of the King's army (page 88, lines 4. 1. 150 - 1). Even better are the attempts by Worcester and Northumberland to shut Hotspurre up, followed by his constantly interrupting them as they try to plan their next course of action (pages 18 - 22).

In addition there is a fine example of what Flatter [23] would suggest are not shared lines but lines jumping in one on top of another as Hotspurre, Worcester, Mortimer and Glendower argue over changing the course of the river to make their respective land allotments more equitable:

Glendower	Ile not have it alter'd.	(6)
Hotspurre	Will not you?	(3)
Glendower	No, nor you shall not.	(5)
Hotspurre	Who shall say me nay?	(5)
Glendower	Why, that will I.	(4)

(page 62, lines 3. 1. 124 - 8)

FACTS

In *Casting Shakespeare's Plays* T.J. King,[24] positing that there is no significant difference in casting requirements between Q1 and F, suggests there are 2,857 spoken Q1 lines and that eleven actors can play sixteen principal roles. Three boys each play a principal female role. Eight men can play fifteen smaller speaking roles and six mutes.

The 'CATALOGUE' lists the play as *The First part of King Henry the fourth*, while the header is set as *The First Part of King Henry the Fourth*. The title above the text is *The First Part of Henry the Fourth, with the Life and Death of HENRY Sirnamed HOT-SPURRE*. Page numbers

---

[21] Spevack, M. *A Complete And Systematic Concordance To The Works Of Shakespeare.* (9 vols.) Hildesheim. Georg Holms. 1968 - 1980

[22] Shared split lines are two or more short verse lines, set for two or more characters, which if placed together (as poets, scholars and commentators suggest), would form a single full line of verse: see the General Introduction, pages xii - xv for further discussion.

[23] Flatter was a ground-breaking scholar who was responsible for exploring the possible significance of Shakespeare's theatre-craft, especially as regards the structure of short lines: see, Flatter, Richard. *Shakespeare's Producing Hand.* London: Heinemann. 1948 (reprint)

[24] King, T.J. *Casting Shakespeare's Plays.* Cambridge. Cambridge University Press. 1992

47 and 48 are missing, the text jumping straight from 46 to 49. There are five catch word variations.

Most modern texts accept F1's Act and Scene Division, though some suggest the fight between Dowglas and the disguised Blunt at the end of Act Five Scene 2 (page 107) should be set as a separate scene, do so, and alter the remaining scene numbers accordingly.

Neil Freeman,
Vancouver, B.C.
Canada, 1998

l

RECOMMENDED MODERN TEXTS WITH EXCELLENT SCHOLARLY FOOTNOTES AND RESEARCH

The footnotes in this text are concise, and concentrate either on matters theatrical or choices in word or line structure which distinguish most modern editions and this Folio based text. Items of literary, historical, and linguistic concern have been well researched and are readily available elsewhere. One of the best **research** works in recent years is

Wells, Stanley, and Gary Taylor, eds. *William Shakespeare: A Textual Companion.* Oxford: Clarendon Press, 1987.

In terms of modern **texts,** readers are urged to consult at least one of the following:

Evans, Gwynne Blakemore, Harry Levin, Anne Barton, Herschel Baker, Frank Kermode, Hallet D. Smith, and Marie Edel, eds. *The Riverside Shakespeare.* Copyright © 1974 by Houghton Mifflin Company.

Humphreys, A. R. (ed.). *King Henry IV, part 1.* The Arden Shakespeare. 1960

Dramatis Personæ

KING Henry the IVth

His Supporters	His Sons
the Earle of WESTEMRLAND	PRINCE Henry, known as Hal (the Prince of Wales)
Sir Walter BLUNT	PRINCE JOHN of Lancaster

Friends And Acquaintances Of Prince Hal

Sir John FALSTAFFE

POINES (known as Yedward or Ned)

BARDOLPH

PETO

Mistresse Quickly, HOSTESSE of an Eastcheape Taverne

FRANCIS, a Drawer

a VINTNER

Those Encountered At Or Near A Country Taverne

GADSHILL, a crony of Falstaffe

CARRIERS

CHAMBERLAINE

an OSTLER

TRAVELLERS

Rebels Against King Henry The Ivth

Those Of England	Those In Wales
the Earle of NORTHUMBERLAND, also known as Percy	Owen GLENDOWER
Northumberland's brother, the Earle of WORCESTER	his son-in-law, Lord Edmund MORTIMER
Northumberland's son, HOTSPURRE, also known as Henry Percy	his wife, Glendower's daughter
Hotspurre's LADY, Kate	
Sir Richard VERNON	**Those Of Scotland**
the ArchBishop of YORKE	the Earle of DOWGLAS
Sir MICHELL	

a SERVANT

a SHERIFE

MESSENGERS

Lords, Souldiors

This Cast List has been specially prepared for this edition, and will not be found in the Facsimile

The First Part of Henry the Fourth, with the Life and Death of HENRY Sirnamed HOT-SPURRE

Actus Primus. Scœna Prima

King   So† shaken as we are, so wan with care,
Finde we a time for frighted Peace to pant,
And breath shortwinded accents of new broils
To be commenc'd in Stronds a-farre remote:

5   No more the thirsty entrance of this Soile,
Shall daube her lippes with her owne childrens blood:
No more shall trenching Warre channell her fields,
Nor bruise her Flowrets with the Armed hoofes
Of hostile paces.

10   Those opposed eyes,
Which like the Meteors of a troubled Heaven,
All of one Nature, of one Substance bred,
Did lately meete in the intestine shocke,
And furious cloze of civill Butchery,

15   Shall now in mutuall well-beseeming rankes
March all one way, and be no more oppos'd
Against Acquaintance, Kindred, and Allies.

The edge of Warre, like an ill-sheathed knife,
No more shall cut his Master.

20   Therefore Friends,
As farre as to the Speulcher of Christ,
Whose Souldier now under whose blessed Crosse
We are impressed and ingag'd to fight,
Forthwith a power of English shall we levie,

25   Whose armes were moulded in their Mothers wombe,

SD ₁ though not included in Qq/Ff, some modern texts add Sir Walter Blunt to the group entry, others wait until the King brings/calls him forward, page 3, lines 65-6 this script

1

To chace these Pagans in those holy Fields,
Over whose Acres walk'd those blessed feete
Which fourteene hundred yeares ago were nail'd
For our advantage on the bitter Crosse.

30 But this our purpose is a twelvemonth old,[1]
And bootlesse 'tis to tell you we will go :
Therefore we meete not now.
                                    Then let me heare
Of you my gentle Cousin Westmerland,
35 What yesternight our Councell did decree,
In forwarding this deere expedience.

Westmerland My Liege : This haste was hot in question,
And many limits of the Charge set downe
But yesternight : when all athwart there came
40 A Post from Wales, loaden with heavy Newes ;
Whose worst was, That the Noble Mortimer,
Leading the men of Herefordshire to fight
Against the irregular and wilde Glendower,
Was by the rude hands of that Welshman taken,
45 And [2] a thousand of his people butchered :   L 46 - b
Upon whose dead corpes there was such misuse,
Such beastly, shamelesse transformation,
By those Welshwomen done, as may not be
(Without much shame) re-told or spoken of.

50 **King** It seemes then, that the tidings of this broile,
Brake off our businesse for the Holy land.

Westmerland This matcht with other like,[3] my gracious Lord,
Farre[4] more uneven and unwelcome Newes
Came from the North, and thus it did report : [5]
55 On Holy-roode day, the gallant Hotspurre there,
Young Harry Percy, and brave Archibald,
That ever-valiant and approoved Scot,
At Holmeden met,° where they did spend
A sad and bloody houre : ° [6]

W[1] Q1 - 3 and most modern texts = 'now is twelve month', Q4 - 5 = 'is twelve month', Ff = 'is a twelvemonth'

W[2] Qq do not set 'And', thus maintaining a 10 syllable line (implying 'butch/er/ed' should equal a full 3 syllable count)

W[3] Q1 - 2 and some modern texts = 'did', Q3 - 5/Ff = 'like'

W[4] Q1 - 4 and most modern texts = 'For', Q5/F1 - 2 = 'Farre'

W[5] Q1 - 4 and most modern texts = 'import', Q5/F1 - 2 = 'report'

LS[6] though Qq/Ff set the passage as three irregular lines (9 - 11/8/6/ syllables) thus allowing Westmerland some

60   As by discharge of their Artillerie,
                     And shape of likely-hood the newes was told :
                     For he that brought them, in the very heate
                     And pride of their contention, did take horse,
                     Uncertaine of the issue any way.

65   **King**   Heere is a deere and true[1] industrious friend,
                     Sir Walter Blunt, new lighted from his Horse,
                     Strain'd[2] with the variation of each soyle,
                     Betwixt that Holmedon, and this Seat of ours :
                     And he hath brought us smooth and welcome[†3] newes.

70   The Earle of Dowglas is discomfited,
                     Ten thousand bold Scots, two and twenty Knights
                     Balk'd in their owne blood did Sir Walter see
                     On Holmedons Plaines.
                                    Of Prisoners, Hotspurre tooke
75   Mordake[4] Earl of Fife, and eldest sonne
                     To beaten Dowglas, and the Earle of Atholl,
                     Of Murry, Angus, and Menteith.

                And is not this an honourable spoyle?
                     A gallant prize?
80   Ha Cosin, is it not?
                Infaith it is.[5]

   Westmerland   A Conquest for a Prince to boast of.

   King   Yea, there thou mak'st me sad, & mak'st me sin,
                     In envy, that my Lord Northumberland
85   Should be the Father of[6] so blest a Sonne :
                     A Sonne, who is the Theame of Honors tongue ;
                     Among'st a Grove, the very straightest Plant,
                     Who is sweet Fortunes Minion, and her Pride :
                     Whil'st I by looking on the praise of him,
90   See Ryot and Dishonor staine the brow
                     Of my yong Harry.
                              O that it could be prov'd,

---

pauses (careful pussyfooting perhaps) around the deeds of Hotspurre, some modern texts reduce the irregularity to just one of two lines (13 - 15/10 syllables) as shown, creating a rather peculiar rush on the first line

R 46 - b : 1. 1. 57 - 86

W [1] Q1 - 4 = 'a true', Q5/Ff = 'and true'

W [2] Qq/F2 = 'Staind', F1 = 'Strain'd'

W [3] Qq/F2/most modern texts = 'welcom', F1 = 'welcomes'

LS [4] though Qq/Ff set an irregular (9 syllable line) as Hotspurre's conquests are mentioned, some modern texts have normalised the moment by adding 'the', thus creating pentameter where none existed before

LS [5] Qq/Ff set this as the last phrase for the King: one commentator/at least one modern text suggests adding this to the opening of Westmerland's reply

W [6] Q1 - 4/F2/most modern texts = 'to', Q5/F1 = 'of'

95		That some Night-tripping-Faiery, had exchang'd In Cradle-clothes, our Children where they lay, And call'd mine Percy, his Plantagenet: Then would I have his Harry, and he mine: But let him from my thoughts.	R 46 - b

That some Night-tripping-Faiery, had exchang'd
In Cradle-clothes, our Children where they lay,
95 And call'd mine Percy, his Plantagenet: R 46 - b
Then would I have his Harry, and he mine:
But let him from my thoughts.
                                    What thinke you Coze
Of this young Percies pride?
100   The Prisoners
Which he in this adventure hath surpriz'd,
To his owne use he keepes, and sends me word
I shall have none but Mordake Earle of Fife.

Westmerland   This is his Unckles teaching.
105   This is Worcester [1]
Malevolent to you in all Aspects:
Which makes him prune himselfe, and brisle up
The crest of Youth against your Dignity.

King   But I have sent for him to answer this:
110 And for this cause a-while we must neglect
Our holy purpose to Jerusalem.

> Cosin, on Wednesday next, our Councell we° will hold
> At Windsor, and so informe the Lords: °[2]

But come your selfe with speed to us againe,
115 For more is to be said, and to be done,
Then out of anger can be uttered.

Westmerland   I will my Liege.

[Exeunt]

PCT [1]   F1 - 3 set no punctuation, as if Westmerland rushes on to complete the idea: Qq/F4/most modern texts set a comma

LS [2]   the Qq/Ff irregularity (11 or 12/9 syllables) suggests that the King's decision is somewhat unusual, most modern texts attempt to regularise the moment by omitting the word 'and' and restructuring as shown (9 or 10/10 syllables)

Scæna Secunda

ENTER HENRY PRINCE OF WALES, SIR JOHN FAL-
STAFFE AND POINTZ [1]

Falstaffe	Now Hal, what time of day is it Lad?
Prince	Thou art so fat-witted with drinking of olde
	Sacke, and unbuttoning thee after Supper, and sleeping
	upon Benches in the afternoone,[2] that thou hast forgotten

5 to demand that truely, which thou wouldest truly know.

What a divell hast thou to do with the time of the day?
unlesse houres were cups of Sacke, and minutes Capons,
and clockes the tongues of Bawdes, and dialls the signes
of Leaping-houses, and the blessed Sunne himselfe a faire
10 hot Wench in Flame-coloured Taffata;   I see no reason,
why thou shouldest bee so superfluous, to demaund the
time of the day.

Falstaffe	Indeed you come neere me now Hal, for we that
	take Purses, go by the Moone and [3] seven Starres, and not

15 by Phœbus hee, that wand'ring Knight so faire. [4]

And I
prythee sweet Wagge, when thou art [5] King, as God save
thy Grace, Majesty I should say, for Grace thou wilte
have none.

20 **Prince**	What, none?
Falstaffe	No, [6] not so much as will serve to be Prologue to
	an Egge and Butter.

N/P/SD 1 Ff's entry refers to the character as 'Pointz', a spelling perhaps used once in dialogue (see footnote #1, page
9): he is referred to in the dialogue both as 'Poynes' and as 'Poines', the latter being the prefix this text will use:
most modern texts omit him from the group entry, and bring him in at about line 129, page 9 this text

W 2 Qq and most modern texts = 'after noon', Ff = 'in the afternoone'

W 3 most modern texts follow Q1 - 4 and add 'the'

SD 4 some modern texts place the phrase 'by Phœbus hee, that wand'ring Knight so faire' in italics or within
quotation marks, suggesting it is taken from a (now lost) contemporary ballad: see *The Arden King Henry Fourth
Part One*, op. cit., footnote to line 15, page 10

W 5 Q2/some modern texts add 'a': Ff omit the word

O 6 most modern texts follow Qq and set the oath omitted by Ff, ', no by my troth,'

5

	Prince	Well, how then?

Come roundly, roundly.

25 **Falstaffe** Marry then, sweet Wagge, when thou art King,
let not us that are Squires of the Nights bodie, bee call'd
Theeves of the Dayes beautie.

Let us be Dianaes Forre-
sters, Gentlemen of the Shade, Minions of the Moone;
30 and let men say, we be men of good Government, being
governed as the Sea is, by our noble and chast mistris the
Moone, under whose countenance we steale.

Prince Thou say'st well, and it holds well too : for the
fortune of us that are the Moones men, doeth ebbe and
35 flow like the Sea, beeing governed as the Sea is, by the
Moone : as for proofe.

[1] Now a Purse of Gold most reso-
lutely snatch'd on Monday night, and most dissolutely
spent on Tuesday Morning ; got with swearing, Lay by :
40 and spent with crying, Bring in : now, in as low an ebbe
as the foot of the Ladder, and by and by in as high a flow
as the ridge of the Gallowes.   L 49 [2] - b

Falstaffe [3] Thou say'st true Lad : and is not my Hostesse of
the Taverne a most sweet Wench?

45 **Prince** As is the hony,[4] my old Lad of the Castle : and is
not a Buffe Jerkin a most sweet robe of durance?

Falstaffe How now? how now mad Wagge?

What in thy
quips and thy quiddities?[+5]
50 What a plague have I to doe
with a Buffe-Jerkin?

Prince Why, what a poxe have I to doe with my Hostesse at the Taverne?

Falstaffe Wll, thou hast call'd her to a reck'ning many a
55 time and oft.

PCT [1]
    Qq/Ff set the 'Now' as the start of a new sentence as shown here, viz. 'as for proofe. Now': however,
some modern texts spoil the homily like quality of the new sentence by removing the period and allowing the
sentence to run on, viz. 'as for proof now . . .'
COMP [2]
    in strict order, this Folio page from which this text comes should be numbered as '47' not '49': however,
within the History section of the First Folio, the page numbers '47' and '48' are omitted
O [3] most modern texts follow Qq and set the oath omitted by Ff, 'By the Lord,'
W [4] Qq/most modern texts add 'of Hibla', Ff omit the phrase
W [5] F1 = 'quid dities', F2/most modern texts = 'quiddities'

	Prince	Did I ever call for thee to pay thy part?
	Falstaffe	No, Ile give thee thy due, thou hast paid al there.
	Prince	Yea and elsewhere, so farre as my Coine would stretch, and where it would not, I have us'd my credit.

60	**Falstaffe**	Yea, and so us'd it, that were it [1] heere apparant,
		that thou art Heire apparant.
		                              But I prythee sweet Wag,
		shall there be Gallowes standing in England when thou
		art King? and resolution thus fobb'd as it is, with the ru-
		stie curbe of old Father Anticke the Law?
		                              Doe not thou
		when thou art a [2] King, hang a Theefe.

65		
	Prince	No, thou shalt.

	Falstaffe	Shall I?
		          O rare!
		                    [3] Ile be a brave Judge.

70		
	Prince	Thou judgest false already. I meane, thou shalt have the hanging of the Theeves, and so become a rare Hangman.
75		
	Falstaffe	Well Hal, well : and in some sort it jumpes with my humour, as well as waiting in the Court, I can tell you.
	Prince	For obtaining of suites?
80	**Falstaffe**	Yea, for obtaining of suites, whereof the Hang- man hath no leane Wardrobe. [4] I am as Melancholly as a Gyb Cat, or a lugg'd Beare.
	Prince	Or an old Lyon, or a Lovers Lute.
85	**Falstaffe**	Yea, or the Drone of a Lincolnshire Bagpipe.
	Prince	What say'st thou to a Hare, or the Melancholly of Moore-Ditch?

R 49 - b : 1. 2. 51 - 78

▼ [1] most modern texts follow Qq and set 'not', which Ff have omitted

▼ [2] most modern texts follow Q1-3 and omit 'a', which is set in Q4 - 5/Ff

○ [3] most modern texts follow Qq and set the oath omitted by Ff, 'By the Lord,'

○ [4] most modern texts follow Qq and set the oath omitted by Ff, 'Zbloud,'

Falstaffe	Thou hast the most unsavoury smiles,[1] and art in- deed the most comparative rascallest [2] sweet yong Prince.
90	But Hal, I prythee trouble me no more with vanity, I wold [3] thou and I knew, where a Commodity of good names were to be bought: an olde Lord of the Councell rated me the other day in the street about you sir; but I mark'd him not, and yet hee talk'd very wisely, but I regarded 95 him not, and yet he talkt wisely, and in the street too.
Prince	Thou didst well: [4] for no man regards it.

Falstaffe	O, thou hast damnable iteration, and art indeede
	able to corrupt a Saint. Thou hast done much harme un-
	to[5] me Hall, God forgive thee for it.
	                                  Before I knew thee
	Hal, I knew nothing: and now I am[6] (if a man shold speake
	truly) little better then one of the wicked.
	                                     I must give o-
	ver this life, and I will give it over: [7] and I do not, I am a
	Villaine.
	                Ile be damn'd for never a Kings sonne in Chri-
	stendome.

Prince	Where shall we take a purse to morrow, Jacke?
110 **Falstaffe**	[8] Where thou wilt Lad, Ile make one: and I doe not, call me Villaine, and baffle me.
Prince	I see a good amendment of life in thee: From Praying, to Purse-taking.
Falstaffe 115	Why, Hal, 'tis my Vocation Hal: 'Tis no sin for a man to labour in his Vocation. [9]

▼ 1 most modern texts follow Q4/F2 and set 'similes', Q1 - 3/Q5/F1 = 'smiles'

▼ 2 Q1 - 3 and most modern texts = 'rascalliest', Q4 - 5/Ff = 'rascallest'

O 3 most modern texts follow Qq and set the oath omitted by Ff, 'to God'

Q 4 most modern texts add from Qq 'for wisdome cries out in the streets and', which is omitted by Ff

▼ 5 Q1 = 'upon', Q2-5/Ff = 'unto'

▼ 6 Qq and most modern texts = 'am I', Ff = 'I am'

O 7 most modern texts follow Qq and set the oath omitted by Ff, 'by the Lord,'

O 8 most modern texts follow Qq and set the oath omitted by Ff, 'Zounds,'

SD 9 Qq/most modern texts set an entry for Poines, rather than Ff's (group) entry at the top of the scene

Poines	[1] Now shall wee know if Gads hill have set a
	Watch. [2]
	O, if men were to be saved by merit, what hole
	in Hell were hot enough for him?
120	This is the most omni
	potent Villaine, that ever cryed, Stand, to a true man.
Prince	Good morrow Ned. R 49 - b
Poines	Good morrow sweet Hal.
	What saies Mon-
125	sieur Remorse?
	What sayes Sir John Sacke and Sugar:
	Jacke?
	How agrees the Divell and thee about thy Soule,
	that thou soldest him on Good-Friday last, for a Cup of
130	Madera, and a cold Capons legge?
Prince	Sir John stands to his word, the divel shall have
	his bargaine, for he was never yet a Breaker of Proverbs:
	He will give the divell his due.
Poines	Then art thou damn'd for keeping thy word with
135	the divell.
Prince	Else he had [3] damn'd for cozening the divell.
Poines	But my Lads, my Lads, to morrow morning, by
	foure a clocke early at Gads hill, there are Pilgrimes go-
	ing to Canterbury with rich Offerings, and Traders ri-
140	ding to London with fat Purses.
	I have vizards for you
	all; you have horses for your selves: Gads-hill lyes to
	night in Rochester, I have bespoke Supper to morrow [4] in
	Eastcheape; we may doe it as secure as sleepe: if you will
145	go, I will stuffe your Purses full of Crownes: if you will
	not, tarry at home and be hang'd.
Falstaffe	Heare ye Yedward, if I tarry at home and go not,
	Ile hang you for going.
Poines	You will chops.
150 Falstaffe	Hal, wilt thou make one?

W/P/SD [1] where this text sets the prefix Poines, Q1 - 3/F2/most modern texts set 'Pointz' as part of Falstaffe's
speech, as if he were calling for him: Q4 - 5/F1 set it as a prefix, also spelling it as 'Pointz'

W [2] Qq and most modern texts = 'match', Ff = 'Watch'

W [3] most modern texts follow Qq/F2 and set 'bin', omitted by F1

W [4] most modern texts follow Qq and set 'night', omitted by Ff

Prince	Who, I rob? ' I a Theefe? Not I. [1]	

155

Falstaffe	There's neither honesty, manhood, nor good fel- lowship in thee, nor thou cam'st not of the blood-royall, if thou dar'st not stand for ten shillings.

Prince	Well then, once in my dayes Ile be a mad-cap.

Falstaffe	Why, that's well said.

Prince	Well, come what will, Ile tarry at home.

160

Falstaffe	[2] Ile be a Traitor then, when thou art King.

Prince	I care not.

Poines	Sir John, I prythee leave the Prince & me alone, I will lay him downe such reasons for this adventure, that he shall go.

165

Falstaffe	Well, maist thou have [3] the Spirit of perswasion; and he [4] the eares of profiting, that what thou speakest, may move; and what he heares may be beleeved, that the true Prince, may (for recreation sake) prove a false theefe; for the poore abuses of the time, want countenance. Far- well, you shall finde me in Eastcheape.

170

Prince	Farwell the latter Spring. Farewell Alhollown Summer. [5]

175

Poines	Now, my good sweet Hony Lord, ride with us to morrow. I have a jest to execute, that I cannot man- nage alone. Falstaffe, Harvey, Rossill,[6] and Gads-hill, shall robbe those men that wee have already way-layde, your

180

O [1] most modern texts follow Qq and set the oath omitted by Ff, 'by my faith.'

O [2] most modern texts follow Qq and set the oath omitted by Ff, 'By the Lord'

O [3] most modern texts set the oath found in Qq 'God give thee', Ff = 'maist thou have'

W [4] Qq/some modern texts = 'him', Ff = 'he'

SD [5] most modern texts add F2's exit for Falstaffe

N/P [6] though listed here in Qq/Ff, the two characters Harvey and Rossill never appear in the play: thus most modern texts replace these names with Bardolph and Peto, characters who participate in the robbery, though at least one modern text consistently assigns lines (usually Peto's) to Harvey: commentators urging the setting of Rossill usually suggest the modern equivalent of 'Russell' be used

selfe and I, wil not be there : and when they have the booty, if you and I do not rob them, cut this head [1] from my
shoulders.

Prince	But [2] how shal we part with them in setting forth?
185 **Poines**	Why, we wil set forth before or after them, and appoint them a place of meeting, wherin it is at our plea-sure to faile ; and then will they adventure uppon the ex-ploit themselves, which they shall have no sooner atchie-ved, but wee'l set upon them.
190 **Prince**	I,[3] but tis like that they will know us by our horses, by our habits, and by every other appointment to be our selves.
Poines	Tut our horses they shall not see, Ile tye them in the wood, our vizards we will change after wee leave 195 them : and sirrah, I have Cases of Buckram for the nonce, to immaske our noted outward garments.
Prince	[4] But I doubt they will be too hard for us.
Poines	Well, for two of them, I know them to bee as L 50 - b true bred Cowards as ever turn'd backe : and for the third 200 if he fight longer then he sees reason, Ile forswear Armes.
	The vertue of this Jest will be, the incomprehensible lyes that this [5] fat Rogue will tell us, when we meete at Supper : how thirty at least he fought with, what Wardes, what blowes, what extremities he endured ; and in the reproofe 205 of this, lyes [6] the jest.
Prince	Well, Ile goe with thee, provide us all things necessary, and meete me to morrow night in Eastcheape, there Ile sup. Farewell.
210 **Poines**	Farewell, my Lord.

[Exit Pointz]

[1] some modern texts add 'off' from Q1-2

[2] most modern text follow Qq and do not print 'But' as set by Ff

[3] Qq and some modern texts = 'Yea', Ff = 'I'

[4] some modern texts follow Qq and print 'Yea' omitted by Ff

[5] Q1 - 4 and most modern texts add 'same', omitted by Q5/Ff

[6] some modern texts follow Q1 and set 'lives', Q2 - 5/Ff = 'lyes'

Prince   I know you all, and will a-while uphold
The unyoak'd humor of your idlenesse:
Yet heerein will I imitate the Sunne,
Who doth permit the base contagious cloudes
215   To smother up his Beauty from the world,
That when he please againe to be himselfe,
Being wanted, he may be more wondred at,
By breaking through the foule and ugly mists
Of vapours, that did seeme to strangle him.

220   If all the yeare were playing holidaies,
To sport, would be as tedious as to worke;
But when they seldome come, they wisht-for come,
And nothing pleaseth but rare accidents.

So when this loose behaviour I throw off,
225   And pay the debt I never promised;
By how much better then my word I am,
By so much shall I falsifie mens hopes,
And like bright Mettall on a sullen ground:
My reformation glittering o're my fault,
230   Shall shew more goodly, and attract more eyes,
Then that which hath no soyle[†1] to set it off.

Ile so offend, to make offence a skill,
Redeeming time, when men thinke least I will. [2]

[†1] Q1 - 3 and most modern texts = 'foile', Q4 - 5 = 'soile', F2= 'soyle', F1 = 's oyle'

[SD 2] most modern texts follow Qq and add a stage direction for the Prince's exit

Scœna Tertia

**ENTER THE KING, NORTHUMBERLAND, WORCESTER, HOTSPURRE,
SIR WALTER BLUNT, AND OTHERS**

King		My blood hath beene too cold and temperate,
		Unapt to stirre at these indignities,
		And you have found me; for accordingly,
		You tread upon my patience: But be sure,
5		I will from henceforth rather be my Selfe,
		Mighty, and to be fear'd, then my condition
		Which hath beene smooth as Oyle, soft as yong Downe,
		And therefore lost that Title of respect,
		Which the proud soule ne're payes, but to the proud.
10	**Worcester**	Our house (my Soveraigne Liege) little deserves
		The scourge of greatnesse to be used on it,
		And that same greatnesse too, which our owne hands

Have holpe to make so portly.

Northumberland My Lord.

15 **King** Worcester get thee gone: for I do see [1]

Danger and disobedience in thine eye.

O sir, your presence is too bold and peremptory,
And Majestie might never yet endure
The moody Frontier of a servant brow,
20 You have good leave to leave us. When we need
Your use and counsell, we shall send for you. [2]

You were about to speake.

}

Northumberland Yea, my good Lord.   R 50 - b

25 Those Prisoners in your Highnesse [3] demanded,
Which Harry Percy heere at Holmedon tooke,
Were (as he sayes) not with such strength denied

[SP 1] the actor has choice as to which two of these three short lines may be joined as one line of split verse
[SD/WHO 2] most modern texts follow Qq and set a stage direction here for the exit of Worcester, and indicate the King's next line is spoken to Northumberland
[W 3] most modern texts follow Qq/F4 and set 'name', which F1 - 3 omit

As was[1] deliver'd to your Majesty:
Who either through envy,[2] or misprision,
30   Was[3] guilty of this fault; and not my Sonne.

Hotspurre   My Liege, I did deny no Prisoners.

But, I remember when the fight was done,
When I was dry with Rage, and extreame Toyle,
Breathlesse, and Faint, leaning upon my Sword,
35   Came there a certaine Lord, neat and trimly drest;
Fresh as a Bride-groome, and his Chin new reapt,
Shew'd like a stubble Land at Harvest home.

He was perfumed like a Milliner,
And 'twixt his Finger and his Thumbe, he held
40   A Pouncet[†4]-box: which ever and anon
He gave his Nose, and took't away againe:
Who therewith angry, when it next came there,
Tooke it in Snuffe: And still he smil'd and talk'd:
And as the Souldiers bare[5] dead bodies by,
45   He call'd them untaught Knaves, Unmannerly,
To[†6] bring a slovenly unhandsome Coarse
Betwixt the Winde, and his Nobility.

With many Holiday and Lady tearme[7]
He question'd me: Among[8] the rest, demanded
50   My Prisoners, in your Majesties behalfe.

I then, all-smarting, with my wounds being cold,
(To be so pestered with a Popingay)
Out of my Greefe, and my Impatience,
Answer'd (neglectingly) I know not what,
55   He should, or[9] should not: For he made me mad,
To see him shine so briske, and smell so sweet,
And talke so like a Waiting-Gentlewoman,
Of Guns, & Drums, and Wounds: God save the marke;
And telling me, the Soveraign'st thing on earth
60   Was Parmacity, for an inward bruise:

[W][1] Q1 - 4 and some modern texts = 'is', Q5 = 'he', Ff = 'was'

[W][2] some modern texts follow Qq and set 'Either envie therefore', Ff = 'Who either through envy'

[W][3] Q1 - 4 and some modern texts = 'Is', Ff = 'Was'

[W][4] F1 = 'P ouncet', F2/most modern texts = 'Pouncet'

[W][5] Qq and most modern texts = 'bore', Ff = 'bare'

[W][6] F1 = 'T o', F2/most modern texts = 'To'

[W][7] Qq/F2 and most modern texts = 'tearmes', F1 = 'tearme'

[W][8] some modern texts follow Q1 - 2 and set 'amongst', Q3 - 5/Ff = 'among'

[W][9] most modern texts follow Qq and set 'he', which Ff omit

And that it was great pitty, so it was,
That [1] villanous Salt-peter should be digg'd
Out of the Bowels of the harmlesse Earth,
Which many a good Tall Fellow had destroy'd
65   So Cowardly.
            And but for these vile Gunnes,
He would himselfe have beene a Souldier.

This bald, unjoynted Chat of his (my Lord)
Made me to answer [2] indirectly (as I said.)
70   And I beseech you, let not this [3] report
Come currant for an Accusation,
Betwixt my Love, and your high Majesty.

Blunt   The circumstances considered, good my Lord,
What ever [4] Harry Percie then had said,
75   To such a person, and in such a place,
At such a time, with all the rest retold,
May reasonably dye, and never rise
To do him wrong, or any way impeach
What then he said, so he unsay it now.

80   **King**   Why yet [5] doth deny his Prisoners,
But with Proviso and Exception,
That we at our owne charge, shall ransome straight
His Brother-in-Law, the foolish Mortimer,
Who (in [6] my soule) hath wilfully betraid
85   The lives of those, that he did lead to Fight,
Against the [7] great Magitian, damn'd Glendower :
Whose daughter (as we heare) the Earle of March
Hath lately married.
            Shall our Coffers then,
90   Be emptied, to redeeme a Traitor home?

Shall we buy Treason? and indent with Feares,
When they have lost and forfeyted themselves.   L 51 - b

L 51 - b : 1. 3. 62 - 88

[1] Qq and most modern texts = 'This', Ff = 'That'

[2] Qq and some modern texts = 'I answered', Ff = 'Made me to answer'

[3] Q1 = 'his', Q2 - 5/Ff = 'this'

[4] Qq = 'What ere', which most modern texts amend to 'Whate'er', often adding 'Lord': Ff = 'What ever'

[5] most modern texts follow Qq/F2 and set 'he', which F1 omits

[6] Q1 - 2 and most modern texts = 'on', Q3 - 5/Ff = 'in'

[7] Q1 and most modern texts = 'that', Q2 - 5/Ff = 'the'

No: on the barren Mountaine [1] let him sterve:
For I shall never hold that man my Friend,
95   Whose tongue shall aske me for one peny cost
To ransome home revolted Mortimer.

Hotspurre   Revolted Mortimer?

He never did fall off, my Soveraigne Liege,
But by the chance of Warre: to prove that true,
100   Needs no more but one tongue. [2]
                              For all those Wounds,
Those mouthed Wounds, which valiantly he tooke,
When on the gentle Severnes siedgie banke,
In single Opposition hand to hand,
105   He did confound the best part of an houre
In changing hardiment with great Glendower:
Three times they breath'd, and three times did they drink
Upon agreement, or swift Severnes flood;
Who then affrighted with their bloody lookes,
110   Ran fearefully among the trembling Reeds,
And hid his crispe-head in the hollow banke,
Blood-stained with these Valiant Combatants.

Never did base [3] and rotten Policy
Colour her working with such deadly wounds;
115   Nor never could the Noble Mortimer
Receive so many, and all willingly:
Then let him not [4] be sland'red with Revolt.

King   Thou do'st bely him Percy, thou dost bely him;
He never did encounter with Glendower:
120   I tell thee, he durst as well have met the divell alone,
As Owen Glendower for an enemy.

Art thou not asham'd?
                      But Sirrah, henceforth
Let me not heare you speake of Mortimer.
125   Send me your Prisoners with the speediest meanes,
Or you shall heare in such a kinde from me
As will displease *ye. [5]
                My Lord Northumberland,

R 51 - b : 1. 3. 89 - 122

[1] Q1/F4 and most modern texts = 'mountaines', Q2 - 5/F1 - 3 = 'Mountaine'

[2] though Qq set a colon and Ff a period, most modern texts create one sentence and allow it to run on freely removing the punctuation altogether, viz. 'needs no more but one tongue for all those wounds'

[3] Qq and most modern texts = 'bare', Ff = 'base'

[4] Qq = 'not him', Ff = 'him not'

[5] the asterisk will be used throughout this text (without further annotation) to mark a difference in 'sophistication' between the Ff and Qq settings: here F1 sets 'ye' for Qq's 'you': see the Introduction for further details

| | | We License your departure with your sonne, |
| 130 | | Send us your Prisoners, or you'l[1] heare of it. |

[Exit King]

| Hotspurre | And if the divell come and roare for them |
| | I will not send them. |

          I will after straight
And tell him so : for I will ease my heart,
135   Although it be with[2] hazard of my head.

| Northumberland | What? drunke with choller? stay & pause awhile, |
| | Heere comes your Unckle. |

[Enter Worcester][3]

| Hotspurre | Speake of Mortimer? |

Yes,[4] I will speake of him, and let my soule
140   Want mercy, if I do not joyne with him.

In his behalfe,[5] Ile empty all these Veines,
And shed my deere blood drop by drop 'i'th dust,
But I will lift the downfall[6] Mortimer
As high 'i'th Ayre, as this Unthankfull King,
145   As this Ingrate and Cankred Bullingbrooke.

| Northumberland | Brother, the King hath made your Nephew mad[7] |

| Worcester | Who strooke this heate up after I was gone? |

Hotspurre	He will (forsooth) have all my Prisoners :
	And when I urg'd the ransom once againe
150	Of my Wives Brother, then his cheeke look'd pale,
	And on my face he turn'd an eye of death,
	Trembling even at the name of Mortimer.

| Worcester | I cannot blame him : was he not[8] proclaim'd |
| | By Richard that dead is, the next of blood? |

[W] [1] Qq = 'you wil', Ff = 'you'l'

[W] [2] Qq and some modern texts = 'Albeit I make a', Ff = 'Although it be with'

[UE] [3] set to the side of the dialogue rather than centered on a separate line, this unusual entry (probably Playhouse added) might suggest Worcester is trying not to draw attention to himself as he returns (hardly surprising since the King banished him from the room at the beginning of the scene

[O] [4] most modern texts follow Qq and set the oath 'Zounds', replaced in Ff by 'Yes,'

[W] [5] Qq and most modern texts = 'Yea on his part', Ff = 'In his behalfe'

[W] [6] Qq and some modern texts = 'down-trod', F1 - 3 = 'downfall', F4 = 'donfaln'

[PCT] [7] F1 = no punctuation (possibly as if Worcester interrupted him), F2/Qq/most modern texts set a period

[W] [8] Qq = 'not he', Ff = 'he not'

17

155	**Northumberland**	He as : I heàrd the Proclamation, And then it was, when the unhappy King (Whose wrongs in us God pardon) did set forth Upon his Irish Expedition : From whence he intercepted, did returne To be depos'd, and shortly murthered.
160		
	Worcester	And for whose death, we in the worlds wide mouth Live scandaliz'd, and fouly spoken of.
	Hotspurre	But soft I pray you ; did King Richard then Proclaime my brother [1] Mortimer, Heyre to the Crowne?
165		
	Northumberland	He did, my selfe did heare it.
	Hotspurre	Nay then I cannot blame his Cousin King, That wish'd him on the barren Mountaines starv'd. [2] But shall it be, that you that set the Crowne

R 51 - b

Upon the head of this forgetfull man,
And for his sake, wore [3] the detested blot
Of murtherous subornation?
                    Shall it be,
That you a world of curses undergoe,
Being the Agents, or base second meanes,
The Cords, the Ladder, or the Hangman rather?

O pardon, if [4] that I descend so low,
To shew the Line, and the Predicament
Wherein you range under this subtill King. [5]

170

175

180
Shall it for shame, be spoken in these dayes,
Or fill up Chronicles in time to come,
That men of your Nobility and Power,
Did gage them both in an unjust behalfe
(As Both of you, God pardon it, have done)

185
To put downe Richard, that sweet lovely Rose,
And plant this Thorne, this Canker Bullingbrooke?

And shall it in more shame be further spoken,
That you are fool'd, discarded, and shooke off
By him, for whom these shames ye underwent?

V/N [1] most modern texts follow Q1 and add Edmund, Q2 - 5/Ff omit the word, creating an eight syllable line

V [2] Qq = 'starve', Ff = 'starv'd'

V [3] Qq = 'weare', Ff = 'wore'

V [4] Q1 - 4 = 'pardon me,', Q5/Ff = 'pardon, if

JST [5] since a question mark followed by a capital letter does not necessarily denote a new sentence in Elizabethan typography, this passage could be set as anywhere between one and three sentences long: Q1 sets it as one

190   No : yet time serves, wherein you may redeeme
Your banish'd Honors, and restore your selves
Into the good Thoughts of the world againe.

Revenge the geering and disdain'd contempt
Of this proud King, who studies day and night
195   To answer all the Debt he owes unto [1] you,
Even with the bloody Payment of your deaths :
Therefore I say ————
            }
Worcester   Peace Cousin, say no more.

And now I will unclaspe a Secret booke,
200   And to your quicke conceyving Discontents,
Ile reade you Matter, deepe and dangerous,
As full of perill and adventurous Spirit,
As to o're-walke a Current, roaring loud
On the unstedfast footing of a Speare.

205 **Hotspurre**   If he fall in, good night, or sinke or swimme :
Send danger from the East unto the West,
So Honour crosse it from the North to South,
And let them grapple : [2] The blood more stirres
To rowze a Lyon, then to start a Hare.

210 **Northumberland** Imagination of some great exploit,
Drives him beyond the bounds of Patience.

Hotspurre   By heaven, me thinkes it were an easie leap,
To plucke bright Honor from the pale-fac'd Moone,
Or dive into the bottome of the deepe,
215   Where Fadome-line could never touch the ground,
And plucke up drowned Honor by the Lockes :
So he that doth redeeme her thence, might weare
Without Co-rivall, all her Dignities :
But out upon this halfe-fac'd Fellowship.

220 **Worcester**   He apprehends a World of Figures here,
But not the forme of what he should attend :
Good Cousin give me audience for a-while,
       [3] And list to me.

Hotspurre   I cry you mercy.

[W1] Q1 - 4 = 'to you' (a 10 syllable line), Q5 = 'you' (a 9 syllable line), Ff = 'unto you' (an 11 syllable line)

[W2] Q1 - 4 and most modern texts = 'O the' (10 syllables), Q5/Ff = 'The' (9 syllables)

[SP3] the actor has choice as to how the following five short lines may be paired as two lines of split verse: most modern texts follow Qq and remove 'And list to me', the first line ending Worcester's speech, thus pairing the second/third and fourth/fifth lines together

225	**Worcester**	Those same Noble Scottes That are your Prisoners.
	Hotspurre	Ile keepe them all.

By 'heaven, he shall not have a Scot of them :
No, if a Scot would save his Soule, he shall not.   L 52 - b

230   Ile keepe them, by this Hand.

Worcester   You start away,
                         And lend no eare unto my purposes.

                         Those Prisoners you shall keepe.

Hotspurre   Nay, I will ;   that's flat :
235   He said, he would not ransome Mortimer :
                         Forbad my tongue to speake of Mortimer.

                         But I will finde him when he lyes asleepe,
                         And in his eare, Ile holla [1] Mortimer.

                         Nay, Ile have a Starling shall be taught to speake
240   Nothing but Mortimer, and give it him,
                         To keepe his anger still in motion.

Worcester   Heare you Cousin : a word.

Hotspurre   All studies heere I solemnly defie,
                         Save how to gall and pinch this Bullingbrooke,
245   And that same Sword and Buckler Prince of Wales.

                         But that I thinke his Father loves him not,
                         And would be glad he met with some mischance,
                         I would have poyson'd him [2] with a pot of Ale.

Worcester   Farewell Kinsman : Ile talke to you
250   When you are better temper'd to attend.

Northumberland   Why what a Waspe-tongu'd [3] & impatient foole
                         Art thou, to breake into this Womans mood,
                         Tying thine eare to no tongue but thine owne?

Hotspurre   Why look you, I am whipt & scourg'd with rods,
255   Netled, and stung with Pismires, when I heare
                         Of this vile Politician Bullingbrooke.

                         In Richards time :   What de'ye [4] call the place?

---

[1] Q1 - 2 = 'hollow', Q3-4 = 'hollo', Q5 = 'hallow', Ff = 'holla'

[2] Qq = 'him poisoned', Ff = 'poyson'd him'

[3] Q1 = 'waspe-stung', Q2 - 5 = 'waspe-tongue', Ff = 'Waspe-tongu'd'

[4] Qq = 'do you', Ff = 'de'ye'

		A plague *upon't, it is in Gloustershire:
		'Twas, where the madcap Duke his Uncle kept,
260		His Uncle Yorke, where I first bow'd my knee
		Unto this King of Smiles, this Bullingbrooke:
	[1]	When you and he came backe from Ravenspurgh.

Northumberland At Barkley Castle.

Hotspurre You say true:
265 Why what a caudie [2] deale of curtesie,
This fawning Grey-hound then did proffer me.

Looke when his infant Fortune came to age,
And gentle Harry Percy, and kinde Cousin:
O, the Divell take such Couzeners, God forgive me,
270 Good Uncle tell your tale, for [3] I have done.

Worcester Nay, if you have not, *too't againe,
*Wee'l stay your leysure.

Hotspurre I have done insooth. [4]

Worcester Then once more to your Scottish Prisoners.
275 Deliver them up without their ransome straight,
And make the Dowglas sonne your onely meane
For powres in Scotland: which for divers reasons
Which I shall send you written, be assur'd
Will easily be granted [5] you, my Lord.
280 Your Sonne in Scotland being thus imploy'd,†[6]
Shall secretly into the bosome creepe
Of that same noble Prelate, well belov'd,
The Archbishop.

Hotspurre Of Yorke, *is't not?

285 **Worcester** True, who beares hard
His Brothers death at Bristow,[7] the Lord Scroope.

I speake not this in estimation,
As what I thinke might be, but what I know

O [1] most modern texts follow Qq and set the oath omitted by Ff, 'Zbloud,'

W [2] Qq and most modern texts = 'candy', F1 - 2 = 'caudie', F3 - 4 = 'gaudie'

W [3] Ff = 'for' (a 10 syllable line), Qq/most modern texts omit the word, setting a 9 syllable line

O [4] most modern texts follow Qq and set the oath 'Ifaith', Ff = 'insooth'

PCT [5] Qq/Ff set variants of what is shown here: however, some modern texts set a new sentence , viz. 'easily be granted.
You my Lord', arguing that it is Northumberland and not Hotspurre that will become allies with the Archbishop

W [6] F1 = 'impl y'd', F2/most modern texts = 'imploy'd'

N [7] Ff/Qq = 'Bristow', some modern texts set the more recogniseable 'Bristol'

290		Is ruminated, plotted, and set downe,
		And onely stayes but to behold the face
		Of that occasion that shall bring it on.

Hotspurre	I smell it : Upon my life, it will do wond'rous well. [1]

Northumberland	Before the *game's a-foot, thou still let'st slip.

295	**Hotspurre**	Why, it cannot choose but be a Noble plot,	R 52 - b
		And then the power of Scotland, and of Yorke
		To joyne with Mortimer, Ha.

Worcester	And so they shall.

Hotspurre	Infaith it is exceedingly well aym'd.

300	**Worcester**	And 'tis no little reason bids us speed,
		To save our heads, by raising of a Head :
		For, beare our selves as even as we can,
		The King will alwayes thinke him in our debt,
		And thinke, we thinke our selves unsatisfied,
305		Till he hath found a time to pay us home.

And see already, how he doth beginne
To make us strangers to his lookes of love.

Hotspurre	He does, he does ; wee'l be reveng'd on him.

Worcester	Cousin, farewell.
310	No further go in this,

Then I by Letters shall direct your course [2]
When time is ripe, which will be sodainly :
Ile steale to Glendower, and loe,[3] Mortimer,
Where you, and Dowglas, and our powres at once,
315 As I will fashion it, shall happily meete,
To beare our fortunes in our owne strong armes,
Which now we hold at much uncertainty.

Northumberland	Farewell good Brother, we shall thrive, I trust.

Hotspurre	Uncle, adieu : O let the houres be short,
320	Till fields, and blowes, and grones, applaud our sport.

[exit]

[SP][1] most modern texts follow Qq and set this as one line, omitting the word 'wondrous'

[PCT][2] though Qq/Ff continue the sentence, most modern texts insert a period here, thus making Worcester's future actions subject to when 'the time is ripe' rather than his advice

[W][3] most modern texts follow Q1 and set 'Lord', arguing this is the true expansion of Q1's abbreviated 'Lo:' Q2 - 5/Ff = 'loe'

Actus Secundus. Scena Prima

ENTER A CARRIER WITH A LANTERNE IN HIS HAND

1st. Carrier Heigh-ho, 'an't be not foure by the day, Ile be hang'd.
Charles waine is over the new Chimney, and yet our horse not packt.
What Ostler?

Ostler Anon, anon.

1st. Carrier I prethee Tom, beate Cuts Saddle, put a few Flockes in the point: the [1] poore Jade is wrung in the withers, out of all cesse.

ENTER ANOTHER CARRIER

2nd. Carrier Pease and Beanes are as danke here as a Dog, and this [2] is the next way to give poore Jades the Bottes: This house is turned upside downe since Robin the [3] Ostler dyed.

1st. Carrier Poore fellow never joy'd since the price of oats rose, it was the death of him. †[4]

2nd. Carrier I thinke this is [5] the most villanous house in al London rode for Fleas: I am stung like a Tench.

1st. Carrier Like a Tench?
[6] There is ne're a King in Christendome,[7] could be better bit, then I have beene since the first Cocke.

L 53 - b : 2. 1. 1 - 18

W [1] most modern texts (rather peculiarly) follow Qq's omission of 'the', which is set in Ff

W [2] Qq and most modern texts = 'that', Ff = 'this'

W [3] most modern texts follow Qq's omission of 'the', which is set in Ff

W [4] F1 = 'ofhim', F2/most modern texts = 'of him'

W [5] Q1 - 4 = 'be', Q5 = 'to be', Ff = 'is'

O [6] most modern texts follow Qq and set the oath omitted by Ff, 'by the Masse,'

W [7] Qq and most modern texts = 'christen', Ff = 'in Christendome'

2nd. Carrier	Why, you [1] wil allow us ne're a Jourden, and then we leake in your Chimney: and your Chamber-lye breeds Fleas like a Loach.	
25 **1st. Carrier**	What Ostler, come away, and be hangd: come away.	
2nd. Carrier	I have a Gammon of Bacon, and two razes of Ginger, to be delivered as farre as Charing-crosse.	
1st. Carrier	[2] The Turkies in my Pannier are quite starved.	

30	What Ostler?
	        A plague on thee, hast thou never an eye in
	thy head?
	        Can'st not heare?
	        And t'were not as good a [3]	

35	deed as drinke, to break the pate of [4] thee, I am a very Vil- laine. Come and be hang'd, hast no faith in thee?	

ENTER GADS-HILL

Gadshill	Good-morrow Carriers. What's *a clocke?	
40 **Carrier** [5]	I thinke it be two *a clocke.	
Gadshill	I *prethee lend me thy Lanthorne to see my Gel- ding in the stable.	L 53 - b
1st. Carrier	Nay [6] soft I pray ye, I know a trick worth two of that. [7]	
45 **Gadshill**	I prethee lend me thine.	
2nd. Carrier	I, when, canst tell? Lend mee thy Lanthorne *(quoth a) marry Ile see thee hang'd first.	
Gadshill 50	Sirra Carrier: What time do you mean to come to London?	

L 53 - b / R 53 - b : 2. 1. 19 - 42

W [1]
  most modern texts follow Q1 - 4 and set 'they', Q5/Ff = 'you'

O [2]
  most modern texts follow Qq and set the oath omitted by Ff, 'Gods bodie'

W [3]
  Q4 - 5/Ff = 'a', Q1 - 3 do not set the word

W [4]
  Q1 - 4 = 'on', Q5/Ff = 'of'

P [5]
  though Qq do not indicate which Carrier speaks, most modern texts assign the speech to the 1st Carrier

O [6]
  most modern texts follow Qq and set the oath omitted by Ff, 'by God'

O [7]
  Qq/most modern texts add the oath 'yfaith'

| 2nd. Carrier | Time enought to goe to bed with a Candle, I warrant thee. |

Come neighbour Mugges, wee'll call up the Gentlemen, they will along with company, for they
55   have great charge.

[Exeunt]
ENTER CHAMBERLAINE

| Gadshill | What ho, Chamberlaine? |

| Chamberlaine | At hand quoth Pick-purse. |

| Gadshill | That's even as faire, as at hand quoth the Cham-
berlaine : For thou variest no more from picking of Pur-
60 ses, then giving direction, doth from labouring.
                                        Thou
lay'st the plot, how. |

| Chamberlaine | Good morrow Master Gads-Hill, it holds cur-
rant that I told you yesternight.
65   There's a Franklin in the
wilde of Kent, hath brought three hundred Markes with
him in Gold : I heard him tell it to one of his company last
night at Supper ; a kinde of Auditor, one that hath abun-
dance of charge too (God knowes what) they are up al-
70 ready, and call for Egges and Butter.
                                        They will away
presently. |

| Gadshill | Sirra, if they meete not with S. Nicholas Clarks,
Ile give thee this necke. |

75 | Chamberlaine | No, Ile none of it : I 'prythee keep that for the
Hangman, for I know thou worshipst S. Nicholas as tru-
ly as a man of falshood may. |

| Gadshill | What talkest thou to me of the Hangman?
                                        If I
80 hang, Ile make a fat payre of Gallowes.
                                For, if I hang,
old Sir John hangs with mee, and thou 'know'st 'hee's no
Starveling.
                Tut, there are other Trojans that ÿ¹ dream'st
85 not of, the which (for sport sake) are content to doe the
Profession some grace ; that would (if matters should bee
look'd into) for their owne Credit sake, make all Whole. |

AB 1 F1 - 2 = 'ÿ', (printed as such because of lack of column width), F3/most modern texts = 'thou'

90

95

I am joyned with no Foot-land-Rakers, no Long-staffe
six-penny strikers, none of these mad Mustachio-purple-
hu'd-Maltwormes, but with Nobility, and Tranquilitie ;
Bourgomasters, and great Oneyers, such as can holde in,
such as will strike sooner then speake ;   and speake sooner
then drinke, and drinke sooner then pray: and yet [1] I lye,
for they pray continually unto [2] their Saint the Commonwealth ;   or rather, not to [3] pray to her, but prey on her: for
they ride up & downe on her, and make hir their Boots.

Chamberlaine What, the Commonwealth their Bootes?
                                                        Will
she hold out water in foule way?

100 **Gadshill** She will, she will ;   Justice hath liquor'd her.
                                                        We
steale as in a Castle, cocksure: we have the receit of Fern-
seede, we walke invisible.

Chamberlaine Nay,[4] I thinke rather,[5] you are more beholding
105 to the Night, then to the [6] Fernseed, for your walking invisible.

| **Gadshill** Give me thy hand.
Thou shalt have a share in our purpose,[7]
As I am a true man. [8] |

110 **Chamberlaine** Nay, rather let mee have it, as you are a false
Theefe.

Gadshill Goe too: *Homo* is a common name to all men.
Bid the Ostler bring the [9] Gelding out of the stable.
                                                        Fare-
115 well, *ye muddy Knave.

                    [Exeunt]   R 53 - b

[O 1] most modern texts follow Qq and set the oath omitted by Ff, '(zoundes)'

[W 2] Qq/some modern texts = 'to', Ff = 'unto'

[W 3] most modern texts follow Qq and do not print 'to' as set in Ff

[O 4] most modern texts follow Qq and set the oath omitted by Ff, 'by my fayth,'

[W 5] Qq and most modern texts omit Ff's 'rather'

[W 6] F1 = 'then to the Fernseed', Qq omit 'the', F2 - 4 omit 'to'

[W 7] Ff = 'purpose', Qq = 'purchase'

[VP 8] Ff are the only texts to set this as the one verse speech within the scene (4/9/6): arguing white space, most modern texts follow Qq and set the speech as prose

[W 9] Qq and most modern texts = 'my', Ff = 'the'

26

Scæna Secunda

ENTER PRINCE, POYNES, AND PETO [1]

Poines	Come shelter, shelter, I have removed Falstafs Horse, and he frets like a gum'd Velvet.
Prince	Stand close.

ENTER FALSTAFFE

	Falstaffe	Poines, Poines, and be hang'd Poines.
5	**Prince**	Peace ye fat-kidney'd Rascall, what a brawling dost thou keepe.
	Falstaffe	What [2] Poines.
		Hal?
	Prince	He is walk'd up to the top of the hill, Ile go seek
10		him. [3]
	Falstaffe	I am accurst to rob in that Theefe [4] company: that [5] Rascall hath removed my Horse, and tied him I know not where.
15		If I travell but foure foot by the squire further a foote, I shall breake my winde.
		Well, I doubt not but to dye a faire death for all this, if I scape hanging for killing that Rogue, I have forsworne his company hourely any time this two and twenty yeare, [6] & yet I am bewitcht
20		with the Rogues company.

L 54 - b : 2. 2. 1 - 17

SD/P [1] the Ff stage direction is as set: Qq suggest others enter with the additional '& c.': thus at least one text adds Harvey and Rosill to the entry, and has them leave before Falstaffe's entry; it alters line 26, page 28, accordingly, and then has them re-enter with the other 'conspirators' after the stage direction 'They Whistle': other modern texts just add Bardolph to the entry, and have he and Peto stand apart at a distance

W [2] Q1 = 'Wheres', Q2 - 5/Ff 'What'

SD [3] most modern texts add a stage direction here, for the Prince to 'retire'

W [4] Qq/F2/most modern texts = 'theeves', F1 = 'Theefe'

W [5] Qq and most modern texts = 'the', Ff = 'that'

W [6] Q1 = 'yeares', Q2 - 5/Ff = 'yeare'

If the Rascall have not given
me medicines to make me love him, Ile be hang'd; ⁺¹ it could
not be else: I have drunke Medicines.

                                      Poines, Hal, a

25   Plague upon you both.

                           Bardolph, Peto: Ile starve ere I ²
rob a foote further.

                       And 'twere not as good a deede as to ³
drinke, to turne True-man, and to leave these Rogues, I

30   am the veriest Varlet that ever chewed with a Tooth.

Eight yards of uneven ground, is threescore & ten miles
afoot with me: and the stony-hearted Villaines knowe it
well enough.

                    A plague *upon't, when Theeves cannot be

35   true one to another.

                    [They Whistle] ⁴

Whew: a plague light ⁵ upon you all.

                              Give ⁶ my Horse you
Rogues: give me my Horse, and be hang'd.

Prince   Peace ye fat guttes, lye downe, lay thine eare

40   close to the ground, and list if thou can ⁷ heare the tread of
Travellers.

Falstaffe   Have you any Leavers to lift me up again being
downe?

                ⁸ Ile not beare *mine owne flesh so far afoot again,

45   for all the coine in thy Fathers Exchequer.

                                  What a plague
meane ye to colt me thus?

Prince   Thou ly'st, thou art not colted, thou art uncolted.

Falstaffe   I prethee good Prince Hal, help me to my horse,

50   good Kings sonne.

ᵂ ₁ F1 = 'behang'd', F2/most modern texts = 'be hang'd'

ᵂ ₂ Qq and most modern texts = 'ile rob', Ff = 'I rob'

ᵂ ₃ most modern texts follow Qq and do not set 'to', as printed in Ff

ˢᴰ ₄ whatever extra characters modern texts added to the top of the scene are usually brought back in with the Prince and Poines

ᵂ ₅ most modern texts follow Qq and do not set 'light', as printed in Ff

ᵂ ₆ most modern texts follow Qq/F3 and set 'me', omitted in F1 - 2

ᵂ ₇ Q1 = 'canst', Q2 - 5/Ff = 'can'

ᴼ ₈ most modern texts follow Qq and set the oath omitted by Ff, 'zbloud,'

Prince	Out *you Rogue, shall I be your Ostler?	
Falstaffe	Go [1] hang thy selfe in thine owne heire-apparant- Garters: If I be tane, Ile peach for this: and I have not Ballads made on all, and sung to filthy tunes, let a Cup of	
55	Sacke be my poyson: when a jest is so forward, & a foote too, I hate it.	

ENTER GADS-HILL [2]

Gadshill	Stand.	
Falstaffe	So I do against my will.	
Poines	O 'tis our Setter, I know his voyce:	
60	Bardolfe, what newes?	
Bardolph	Case ye, case ye: on with your Vizards, there's mony of the Kings comming downe the hill, 'tis going to the Kings Exchequer.	
Falstaffe	You lie *you rogue, 'tis going to the Kings Tavern.	
65	**Gadshill**	There's enough to make us all.
Falstaffe	To be[†3] hang'd.	L 54 - b
Prince	[4] You foure shall front them in the narrow Lane: Ned [5] and I, will walke lower; if they scape from your en- counter, then they light on us.	
70	**Peto**	But how many be of them? [6]
Gadshill	Some eight or ten.	
Falstaffe	[7] Will they not rob us?	
Prince	What, a Coward Sir John Paunch?	
Falstaffe	Indeed I am not John of Gaunt your Grandfather; but yet no Coward, Hal.	
75		

L 54 - b / R 54 - b : 2. 2. 42 - 68

▼ 1
most modern texts follow Qq and do not set 'Go', as printed in Ff

SD/P 2
as Bardolph is spoken to and replies in three speeches time, most modern texts add his entry here: also since
in four lines time Poines says he recognises the 'Setter's' voyce, some modern texts suggest Gads-hill is masked

▼ 3
F1 = 'he', Qq/F2/most modern texts = 'be'

▼ 4
most modern texts follow Qq and do set 'Sirs', omitted in Ff

▼ 5
most modern texts follow Qq and set 'Poines', omitted in Ff

▼ 6
Q1 = 'How many be there of them?', Q2 = 'How many be they?', Q3 - 5 = 'But how many be they?', Ff = 'But
how many be of them?'

O 7
most modern texts follow Qq and set the oath omitted by Ff, 'Zounds'

Prince	Wee'l [1] leave that to the proofe.
Poines	Sirra Jacke, thy horse stands behind the hedg, when thou need'st him, there thou shalt finde him. Fare
80	well, and stand fast.
Falstaffe	Now cannot I strike him, if I should be hang'd.
Prince	Ned, where are our disguises?
Poines	Heere hard by: Stand close. [2]
Falstaffe	Now my Masters, happy man be his dole, say I:
85	every man to his businesse.

ENTER TRAVELLERS

Traveller	[3] Come Neighbor: the boy shall leade our Horses downe the hill: Wee'l walke a-foot a while, and ease our [4] Legges.
Theeves	Stay. [5]
90 **Traveller{s}**	Jesu [6] blesse us.
Falstaffe	Strike down with them, cut the villains throats; a whorson Caterpillars: Bacon-fed Knaves, they hate us youth; downe with them, fleece them.
Traveller{s}	O, we are undone, both we and ours for ever.
95 **Falstaffe**	Hang ye gorbellied knaves, are *you undone? No
	ye Fat Chuffes, I would your store were heere. On Ba-
100	cons on, what ye knaves? Yong men must live, you are Grand Jurers, are ye? Wee'l jure ye ifaith. [7]

W 1   Q1 - 2 = 'Well, we', Q3 - 5 = 'Well, weele', Ff = 'Wee'l'

SD 2   most modern texts add a stage direction here for the Prince and Poines to exit unnoticed by the rest

P 3   the Ff prefix for these speeches is 'Tra.' throughout, the Q1 prefix is 'Travel.' or 'Tra.': thus, after this speech, which is seems to be the remarks of a single character, the reader may assign the remainder to either a single character, various characters, or to the group as a whole

W 4   Qq/Ff = 'our', one modern texts sets 'their'

W 5   Q1 - 4 = 'Stand', Q5/Ff = 'Stay'

W 6   Qq and most modern texts = 'Jesus', Ff = 'Jesu'

O 7   Q1 - 2 = 'ye faith', Q3 - 5/Ff = 'ye ifaith'

**HEERE THEY ROB THEM, AND BINDE THEM. ENTER THE
PRINCE AND POINES** [1]

Prince	The Theeves have bound the True-men: Now
	could thou and I rob the Theeves, and go merily to Lon-
105	don, it would be argument for a Weeke, Laughter for a
	Moneth, and a good jest for ever.
Poines	Stand close, I heare them comming. [2]

ENTER THEEVES AGAINE

Falstaffe	Come my Masters, let us share, and then to horsse
	before day: and the Prince and Poynes bee not two ar-
110	rand Cowards, there's no equity stirring.

> There's no *moe
> valour in that Poynes, than in a wilde Ducke.

Prince	Your money.
Poines	Villaines.

**AS THEY ARE SHARING, THE PRINCE AND POYNES SET UPON THEM.
THEY ALL RUN AWAY, LEAVING THE BOOTY BEHIND THEM**

115	Prince	Got with much ease.

> Now merrily to Horse: °

> The Theeves are [3] scattred, and possest with fear° so strong-
> ly, that they dare not meet each other: ° each takes his fel-
> low for an Officer. °
>
> Away good Ned, Falstaffe sweates to
> death,° and Lards the leane earth as he walkes along: ° wer't
> not for laughing, I should pitty him. ° [4]

Poines	How the [5] Rogue roar'd.

[Exeunt]

R 54 - b : 2. 2. 93 - 111

SD/ALT [1] most modern texts add the Q1 - 3 direction that Falstaffe's group exits before the Prince and Poines enter,
and suggest that the latter are in disguise: at least one modern text suggests this is a new scene, and numbers it
Act two Scene 3

SD [2] most modern texts add a stage direction for the Prince and Poines to withdraw as the 'Theeves' enter

▼ [3] Q1 and some modern texts = 'all', Q2 - 5/Ff do not set the word

VP [4] though Qq/Ff set the speech as easy prose, several modern texts set verse as shown, which is somewhat
surprising since in Qq/Ff Hal hardly ever uses verse except in Court matters and/or affairs of state, or, as with the
Sheriff later (pages 55-6), when he needs to pull rank

▼ [5] some modern texts follow the Quarto known as (Q) (see the introduction to this text) and add 'fat': Q1-5/Ff do
not set the word

31

Scœna Tertia

ENTER HOTSPURRE SOLUS, READING A LETTER

*But for mine owne part, my Lord, I could bee well contented to
be there, in respect of the love I beare your house.*

R 54 - b

He could be contented: Why is he not then? in[1] respect of
the love he beares our house.

5   He shewes in this, he loves
his owne Barne better then he loves our house.
                                       Let me
see some more.
                      The purpose you undertake is dangerous .

10 Why that's certaine: 'Tis dangerous to take a Colde, to
sleepe, to drinke: but I tell you (my Lord foole) out of
this Nettle, Danger; we plucke this Flower, Safety.
                                            *The
purpose you undertake is dangerous, the Friends you have na-*
15 *med uncertaine, the time it selfe unsorted, and your whole
Plot too light, for the counterpoize of so great an Opposition.*

Say you so, say you so: I say unto you againe, you are a
shallow cowardly Hinde, and you Lye.
                                   What a lacke-
20 braine is this?
                       I protest,[2] our plot is as good a plot[3] as ever
was laid; our Friend true and constant: A good Plotte,
good Friends, and full of expectation: An excellent plot,
very good Friends.
25   What a Frosty-spirited rogue is this?

Why, my Lord of Yorke commends the plot, and the
generall course of the action.
                          By this hand[4], if I were now
by this Rascall, I could braine him with his Ladies Fan.

R 54 - b / L 55 - b : 2. 3. 1 - 23

[1] Qq add 'the', which Ff and some modern texts omit

[2] most modern texts follow Qq and set the oath 'by the Lord': Ff = 'I protest'

[3] Qq = 'a good plot', Ff = 'as good a plot'

[4] most modern texts follow Qq and set the oath 'Zoundes, and': Ff = 'By this hand, if'

30   Is there not my Father, my Unckle, and my Selfe, Lord
Edmund Mortimer, my Lord of Yorke, and Owen Glendour?
Is there not besides, the Dowglas?
                              Have I not all their let-
ters, to meete me in Armes by the ninth of the next Mo-
35   neth? and are they not some of them set forward already?
What a Pagan Rascall is this?
                      An Infidell.
                                Ha, you shall
see now in very sincerity of Feare and Cold heart, will he
40   to the King, and lay open all our proceedings.
                                O, I could
divide my selfe, and go to buffets, for moving such a dish
of skim'd [1] Milk with so honourable an Action.
                                Hang him,
45   let him tell the King we are prepared.
                            I will set *forwards
to night.

ENTER HIS LADY

How now Kate, I must leave you within these two hours.

Lady	O my good Lord, why are you thus alone?
50	For what offence have I this fortnight bin A banish'd woman from my Harries bed?
	Tell me (sweet Lord) what is't that takes from thee Thy stomacke, pleasure, and thy golden sleepe?
55	Why dost thou bend thine eyes upon the earth? And start so often when thou sitt'st alone?
	Why hast thou lost the fresh blood in thy cheekes? And given my Treasures and my rights of thee, To thicke-ey'd musing, and curst mellancholly?
60	In my [2] faint-slumbers, I by thee have watcht, And heard thee murmore tales of Iron Warres: Speake tearmes of manage to thy bounding Steed, Cry courage to the field. [3]

                           And thou hast talk'd

[W1] Qq = 'skim', Ff = 'skim'd'

[W2] most modern texts follow Q1 - 3 and set 'thy', Q4 - 5/Ff = 'my'

[ST3] since up to this point each potential sentence ends at the end of a line, and is followed by a new verse line which traditionally is always set with a capital letter, this opening passage could be set anywhere between one and seven sentences long: this Folio Script shows the passage as five sentences, and readers are invited to make their own final determination: the fewer the sentences chosen the more (emotional) speed will his Lady possess

Of Sallies, and Retires;   Trenches, Tents,
65   Of Palizadoes, Frontiers, Parapets,
Of Basiliskes, of Canon, Culverin,
Of Prisoners ransome,[1] and of Souldiers slaine,
And all the current[2] of a headdy fight.

Thy spirit within thee hath beene so at Warre,
70   And thus hath so bestirr'd thee in thy sleepe,
That beds[3] of sweate hath[4] stood upon thy Brow,
Like bubbles in a late-disturbed Streame;
And in thy face strange motions have appear'd,
Such as we see when men restraine their breath
75   On some great sodaine hast.[5]
                              O what portents are these?

Some heavie businesse hath my Lord in hand,
And I must know it: else he loves me not.

Hotspurre	What ho;[6] Is Gilliams with the Packet gone?	
80	**Servant**	He is my Lord, an houre agone.[7]
	Hotspurre	Hath Butler brought those horses frö the Sheriffe? L 55 - b
	Servant	One horse, my Lord, he brought even now.
	Hotspurre	What Horse?

                    A Roane, a crop eare, is it not.

85   **Servant**   It is my Lord.

Hotspurre   That Roane shall be my Throne.°
                                    Well, I will
backe him straight.
                    [8] *Esperance*,° bid Butler lead him forth
90   into the Parke.° [9] [10]

[W][1] though most modern texts agree with Qq/Ff and print this as 'ransome' one gloss = 'ransom'd'

[W][2] Q1 - 3 = 'currents', Ff = 'current'

[W][3] most modern texts follow Q1 and set 'beads', Q2 - 5/Ff = 'beds'

[W][4] Q1 - 3 = 'have', Q4 - 5/Ff = 'hath'

[W][5] Q1 = 'hest', Q2-3/F3 = 'haste', Q4 - 5/F1 - 2 = 'hast'

[SD][6] most modern texts add a stage direction either before or after this phrase for the entry of the Servant

[W][7] Q1 - 3 and most modern texts = 'ago', Q4 - 5/Ff = 'agone'

[W][8] most modern texts follow Q1 - 4 and add 'O', which is not set in Ff

[SD][9] most modern texts add a stage direction here for the Servant to exit

[VP][10] though Qq/Ff set this passage as prose, most modern texts restructure the passage into verse, even though there is no clear indication, yet, that Hotspurre has spoken verse so far in the scene: by introducing verse now, the modern texts may have diminished the time Qq/Ff definitely set verse for him, at the moment of reply to his wife's challenge to tell the truth, see line 108, page 35

	Lady	But heare you, my Lord.
	Hotspurre	What say'st thou my Lady?
	Lady	What is it carries you away?
	Hotspurre	Why, my horse (my Love) my horse.

95   **Lady**   Out you mad-headed Ape,° a Weazell hath not
such a deale of Spleene,° as you are tost with.
           In sooth° ¹ Ile
know your businesse Harry, that I will. °
           I feare my Bro-
100   ther Mortimer doth stirre° about his Title, and hath sent
for you° to line his enterprize.
           But if you go° ———

     Hotspurre   So farre a foot, I shall be weary, Love. °

     Lady   Come, come, you Paraquito, answer me° directly
105   unto this question, that I shall ² aske. °
           Indeede ³ Ile breake
thy little finger Harry,° if thou wilt not tel me true. ° ⁴ ⁵

	Hotspurre	Away,⁶ away you trifler: Love, I love thee not,
110		I care not for thee Kate: this is no world
		To play with Mammets, and to tilt with lips.

             We must have bloodie Noses, and crack'd Crownes,
And passe them currant too.
           Gods me, my horse.
What say'st thou Kate? what wold'st thou have with me?

115   **Lady**   Do ⁎ye not love me?
           Do ⁎ye not indeed?
Well, do not then.
           For since you love me not,
I will not love my selfe.
120   Do you not love me?

° ₁
   most modern texts follow Qq and set the oath 'In faith', Ff = 'In sooth'

ᵂ ₂
   some modern texts follow Q1 and omit 'shall' which is set by Q2 - 5/Ff

O/PCT ₃
   Ff set 'Indeede', Qq/most modern texts set the oath 'in faith' (plus a comma, so continuing the sentence)

ᵂ ₄
   Qq = 'and if thou wilt not tel me all things true.', Ff = 'if thou wilt not tel me true'

VP ₅
   again, though Qq/Ff set this as prose, most modern texts restructure the passage into verse as shown: see
the final footnote, previous page

LS ₆
   though Qq/Ff set the line as shown (12 syllables), some modern texts rather peculiarly set a separate two
syllable line for the first 'Away'

Nay, tell me if thou speak'st [1] in jest, or no.

Hotspurre   Come, wilt thou see me ride?

And when I am a horsebacke, I will sweare
I love thee infinitely.
125   But hearke you Kate,
I must not have you henceforth, question me,
*Whether I go : nor reason whereabout.

*Whether I must, I must : and to conclude,
This Evening must I leave *thee, gentle Kate.
130   I know you wise, but yet no *further wise
Then Harry Percies wife.
                                   Constant you are,
But yet a woman : and for secrecie,
No Lady closer.
135   For I will [2] beleeve
Thou wilt not utter what thou do'st not know,
And so farre wilt [3] I trust thee, gentle Kate.

Lady   How so farre?

Hotspurre   Not an inch further.
140   But harke you Kate,
Whither I go, thither shall you go too :

To day will I set forth, to morrow you.
Will this content you Kate?
                                         ⟩
Lady   It must of force.

[Exeunt]

▼ 1 Q and most modern texts = 'you speake', Ff = 'thou speak'st'
▼ 2 Q1 - 3 = 'well', Q4 = 'wil', Q5/Ff = 'will'
▼ 3 Q1-4/F2 - 4 = 'far will', F1 = 'farre wilt'

Scena Quarta

ENTER PRINCE AND POINES

Prince	Ned, prethee come out of that fat roome, & lend me thy hand to laugh a little.
Poines	Where hast bene Hall? [1]
Prince	With three or foure Logger-heads, amongst 3.

5 or foures core Hogsheads.
                              I have sounded the verie base
string of humility.
                              Sirra, I am sworn brother to a leash of
Drawers, and can call them [2] by their [3] names, as Tom, Dicke,
10 and Francis.
                              They take it already upon their confidence, [4]
that though I be but Prince of Wales, yet I am the King
of Curtesie : telling me flatly I am no [5] proud Jack like Falstaffe, but a Corinthian, a lad of mettle, a good boy, [6] and
15 when I am King of England, I shall command al the good
Laddes in East-cheape.
                              They call drinking deepe, dy-
ing Scarlet ; and when you breath in your watering, then [7]   R 55 - b
they cry hem, and bid you play it off.
20   To conclude, I am
so good a proficient in one quarter of an houre, that I can
drinke with any Tinker in his owne Language during my
life.
                              I tell thee Ned, thou hast lost much honor, that thou
25 wer't not with me in this action : but sweet Ned, to swee-
ten which name of Ned, I give thee this peniworth of Su-

R 55 - b / L 56 - b : 2. 4. 1 - 23

N/W 1 Qq/most modern texts = 'Hal', Ff = 'Hall'

W 2 most modern texts follow Qq and set 'all', omitted by Ff

W 3 most modern texts follow Qq and set 'christen' (i.e. 'Christian'), omitted by Ff

W 4 Qq and most modern texts = 'salvation', Ff = 'confidence'

W 5 most modern texts follow Q4 - 5 and set 'and tel me flatly I am not proud', F1 = 'telling me flatly I am no proud', with F2 - 4 substituting 'not' for F1's 'no'

O 6 most modern texts follow Qq and set the oath omitted by Ff, '(by the Lord so they call me)'

W 7 most modern texts follow Qq and omit 'then', set by Ff

gar, clapt even now into my hand by an under Skinker,
one that never spake other English in his life, then *Eight*
shillings and six pence , and, *You are welcome* :   with this shrill
30   addition, *Anon, Anon sir, Score a Pint of Bastard in the*
Halfe Moone, or so .
          But Ned, to drive away [1] time till Fal-
staffe come, I prythee doe thou stand in some by-roome,
while I question my puny Drawer, to what end hee gave
35   me the Sugar, and do [2] never leave calling Francis, that his
Tale to me may be nothing but, Anon: step aside, and Ile
shew thee a President. [3]

Poines	Francis.	
Prince	Thou art perfect.	
40 **Poines**	Francis.	

ENTER DRAWER

Francis	Anon, anon sir; looke downe into the Pomgar- net, Ralfe.
Prince	Come hither Francis.
Francis	My Lord.
45 **Prince**	How long hast thou to serve, Francis?
Francis	Forsooth five yeares, and as much as to ————
Poines	Francis.
Francis	Anon, anon sir.
Prince	Five yeares: [4] Berlady a long Lease for the clin- 50 king of Pewter. But Francis, darest thou be so valiant, as to play the coward with thy Indenture, & shew it a faire paire of heeles, and run from it?
Francis 55	O Lord sir, Ile be sworne upon all the [5] Books in England, I could finde in my heart.

---

[1] most modern texts follow Q1 - 3 and set 'the', omitted by Q4 - 5/Ff

[2] most modern texts follow Q1 - 3 and set 'thou', omitted by Q4 - 5/Ff

[3] most modern texts add a stage direction that Poines withdraws and then continues to call from 'within'

[4] Q1 - 2 = 'yeare', Q3 - 5/Ff = 'yeares'

[5] most modern texts follow Q1 - 3/Ff and set 'the', omitted by Q4 - 5

Poines	Francis.
Francis	Anon, anon [1] sir.
Prince	How old art thou, Francis?
Francis	Let me see, about Michaelmas next I shal be[†2] ——
60 **Poines**	Francis.
Francis	Anon sir, pray you [3] stay a little, my Lord.
Prince	Nay but harke you Francis, for the Sugar thou gavest me, 'twas a penyworth, was't not?
Francis	O Lord sir,[4] I would it had bene two.
65 **Prince**	I will give thee for it a thousand pound: Aske me when thou wilt, and thou shalt have it.
Poines	Francis.
Francis	Anon, anon.
Prince	Anon Francis?
70	No Francis, but to morrow Francis: or Francis, on* thursday: or indeed Francis when thou wilt. But Francis.
Francis	My Lord.
75 **Prince**	Wilt thou rob this LeatherneJerkin, Christall button, Not-pated, Agat ring, Pukestocking, Caddice garter, Smooth tongue, Spanish pouch.
Francis	O Lord sir, who do you meane?
Prince	Why then your browne Bastard is your onely drinke: for looke you Francis, your white Canvas doublet will sulley.
80	In Barbary sir, it cannot come to so much.
Francis	What sir?

L 56 - b : 2. 4. 51 - 76

[1] most modern texts follow Qq and omit the second 'anon', added by Ff

[2] F1 = 'shalbe', F2/most modern texts = 'shall be'

[3] most modern texts follow Q1 and set 'you', omitted by Q2 - 5/Ff

[4] most modern texts follow Qq and omit 'sir', added by Ff

39

Poines	Francis.	
85	**Prince**	Away you Rogue, dost thou [1] heare them call?

**HEERE THEY BOTH CALL HIM, THE DRAWER STAND AMAZED,
NOT KNOWING WHICH WAY TO GO**

ENTER VINTNER

Vintner	What, stand'st thou still, and hear'st such a cal-ling?

L 56 - b

      Looke to the Guests within. [2]

                My Lord, Olde Sir

90   John with halfe a dozen more, are at the doore :   shall I let
them in?

Prince	Let them alone awhile, and then open the doore. [3]

Poines.

ENTER POINES

Poines	Anon, anon sir.
95 **Prince**	Sirra, Falstaffe and the rest of the Theeves, are at the doore, shall we be merry?
Poines	As merrie as Crickets my Lad.

                    But harke yee,
What cunning match have you made with this jest of the
100   Drawer?

               Come, what's the issue?

Prince	I am now of all humors, that have shewed them-selves humors, since the old dayes of goodman Adam, to the pupill age of this present twelve a clock at midnight. [4]

105   What's 'a clocke Francis?

Francis	Anon, anon sir.

ᵂ [1] most modern texts follow Q1 - 3 and set 'not', omitted by Q4 - 5/Ff

ˢᴰ [2] most modern texts add a stage direction here for the exit of Francis

ˢᴰ [3] most modern texts add a stage direction here for the Vintner's exit

ˢᴰ [4] most modern texts add two stage directions, one before this sentence for the entry of Francis, the other, after his reply, for his exit

Prince	That ever this Fellow should have fewer words

Prince — That ever this Fellow should have fewer words
then a Parret, and yet the sonne of a Woman.

His indu-
110   stry is up-staires and down-staires, his eloquence the parcell of a reckoning.

* I am not yet of Percies mind, the Hot-
spurre of the North, he that killes me some sixe or seauen
dozen of Scots at a Breakfast, washes his hands, and saies
115   to his wife ; Fie upon this quiet life, I want worke.

O my
sweet Harry sayes she, how many hast thou kill'd to day?

Give my Roane horse a drench (sayes hee) and answeres,
some fourteene, an houre after : a trifle, a trifle.

120   I prethee
call in Falstaffe, Ile play Percy, and that damn'd Brawne
shall play Dame Mortimer his wife, *Rivo*, sayes the drun-
kard.

Call in Ribs, call in Tallow.

ENTER FALSTAFFE [1]

125 Poines   Welcome Jacke, where hast thou beene?

Falstaffe   A plague of all Cowards I say, and a Vengeance
too, marry and Amen.

Give me a cup of Sacke Boy.

Ere
130   I leade this life long, Ile sowe nether stockes, and mend
them [2] too.

A plague of all cowards.

Give me a Cup of
Sacke, Rogue.

135   Is there no Vertue extant?

Prince   Didst thou never see Titan kisse a dish of Butter, pittifull
hearted Titan that melted at the sweete Tale of
the Sunne?

If thou didst, then behold that compound.

140 Falstaffe   You Rogue, heere's Lime in this Sacke too : there
is nothing but Roguery to be found in Villanous man ; yet
a Coward is worse then a Cup of Sack with lime. [3]

[SD] [1] most modern texts add Gadshill, Bardolph, and Peto to the entry, and sometimes Francis with wine

[W] [2] most modern texts follow Qq and set 'and foote them', omitted by Ff

[W] [3] most modern texts follow Qq and set 'in it', omitted by Ff

A vil-
lanous Coward, go thy wayes old Jacke, die when thou
145   wilt, if manhood, good manhood be not forgot upon the
face of the earth, then am I a shotten Herring : there lives
not three good men unhang'd in England, & one of them
is fat, and growes old, God helpe the while, a bad world I
say.
150   I would I were a Weaver, I could sing all manner of
songs. [1]
        A plague of all Cowards, I say still.

Prince   How now Woolsacke, what mutter[2] you?

Falstaffe   A Kings Sonne?
155   If I do not beate thee out of thy
Kingdome with a dagger of Lath, and drive all thy Sub-
jects afore thee like a flocke of Wilde-geese, Ile never
weare haire on my face more.
             You Prince of Wales?

160 **Prince**   Why you horson round man? what's the matter?

Falstaffe   Are you not [3] a Coward?
           Answer me to that, and
Poines there?

Prince   [4] Ye fatch paunch, and yee call mee Coward, [5] Ile
165   stab thee.

Falstaffe   I call thee Coward?
          Ile see thee damn'd ere I call
the [6] Coward : but I would give a thousand pound I could
run as fast as thou canst.
170   You are straight enough in the
shoulders, you care not who sees your backe : Call you   R 56 - b
that backing of your friends? a plague upon such backing : give me them that will face me.
          Give me a Cup
175   of Sack, I am a Rogue if I drunke to day.

L 56 - a (or j) / L 57 - a (or j) : 2. 4. 128 - 152

[W1] Qq and most modern texts = 'I could sing psalmes, or any thing.': Ff = ', I could sing all manner of songs.'

[W2] F1 = 'mntter', F2/most modern texts = 'mutter'

[W3] Q1 = 'not you', Q2 - 5/Ff = 'you not'

[O/W4] most modern texts follow Qq and set the oath 'Zoundes ye fat', F1 - 2 = 'Ye fatch', F3 - 4 = 'Ye fat'

[O5] most modern texts follow Qq and set the oath omitted by Ff, 'by the Lord'

[W6] Qq/F2 and most modern texts = 'thee', Ff = 'the'

	Prince	O Villaine, thy Lippes are scarce wip'd, since thou drunk'st last.
	Falstaffe	*All's one for that.

[He drinkes]

A plague of all Cowards still, say I.

180 | **Prince** | What's the matter?

Falstaffe | What's the matter? here be foure of us,[1] have ta'ne a thousand pound this [2] Morning.

Prince | Where is it, Jack? where is it?

Falstaffe | Where is it? taken from us, it is: a hundred
185 | | upon foure of us.

Prince | What, a hundred, man?

Falstaffe | I am a Rogue, if I were not at halfe Sword with a dozen of them two houres together.
|||I have scaped by
190 | | miracle.
|||I am eight times thrust through the Doublet, foure through the Hose, my Buckler cut through and through, my Sword hackt like a Hand-saw, *ecce signum*. [3]

I never dealt better since I was a man: all would not doe.

195 | | A plague of all Cowards; let them speake; if they speake more or lesse then truth, they are villaines, and the sonnes of darknesse.

Prince | Speake sirs, how was it?

Gadshill | We foure set upon some dozen.

200 | **Falstaffe** | Sixteene, at least, my Lord.

Gadshill | And bound them.

Peto | No, no, they were not bound.

Falstaffe | You Rogue, they were bound, every man of them, or I am a Jew else, an Ebrew Jew.

[W][1] Q1 - 2 = 'there be foure of us here', Q3 - 5/Ff = 'here be foure of us'

[W][2] most modern texts follow Q1 - 2 and set 'day', omitted by Q3 - 5/Ff

[SD][3] some modern texts suggest Falstaffe draws his sword to show how badly it has been 'hackt'

205	**Gadshill**	As we were sharing, some sixe or seven fresh men set upon us.
	Falstaffe	And unbound the rest, and then come in the other.
	Prince	What, fought *yee with them all?
210	**Falstaffe**	All? I know now what *yee call all: but if I fought not with fiftie of them, I am a bunch of Radish: if there were not two or three and fiftie upon poore olde Jack, then am I no two-legg'd Creature.
215	**Poines** [1]	Pray *Heaven, you have not murthered some of them.
	Falstaffe	Nay, that's past praying for, I have pepper'd two of them: Two I am sure I have payed, two Rogues in Buckrom Sutes.
220		I tell thee what, Hal, if I tell thee a Lye, spit in my face, call me Horse: thou knowest my olde word: [2] here I lay, and thus I bore my point; foure Rogues in Buckrom let drive at me.
	Prince	What, foure? thou sayd'st but two, even now.
225	**Falstaffe**	Foure Hal, I told thee foure.
	Poines	I, I, he said foure.
	Falstaffe	These foure came all a-front, and mainely thrust at me; I made [3] no more adoe, but tooke all their seven points in my Targuet, thus. [4]
230	**Prince**	Seven? why there were but foure, even now.
	Falstaffe	In Buckrom.
	Poines	I, foure, in Buckrom Sutes.
	Falstaffe	Seven, by these Hilts, or I am a Villaine else.

[P] [1] most modern texts follow Q1 - 4 and assign this speech to the Prince, Q5/Ff = Poines

[W/SD] [2] Q1 - 4 and most modern texts = 'warde', Q5/Ff = 'word', also some modern texts suggest Falstaffe stands 'as if to fight'

[W] [3] most modern texts follow Q1 - 2 and set 'me', omitted by Q3 - 5/Ff

[SD] [4] some modern texts suggest Falstaffe now takes up his sword and buckler to demonstrate what happened

	Prince	[1] Prethee let him alone, we shall have more anon.
235	Falstaffe	Doest thou heare me, Hal?
	Prince	I, and marke thee too, Jack.
	Falstaffe	Doe so, for it is worth the listning too: these nine in Buckrom, that I told thee of.
	Prince	So, two more alreadie.
240	Falstaffe	Their Points being broken.
	Poines	Downe fell his [2] Hose.
	Falstaffe	Began to give me ground: but I followed me L 57 - a (or j) close, came in foot and hand; and with a thought, seven of the eleven I pay'd.
245	Prince	O monstrous! eleven Buckrom men growne out of two?
	Falstaffe	But as the Devill would have it, three mis-be-gotten Knaves, in Kendall Greene, came at my Back, and let drive at me; for it was so darke, Hal, that thou could'st
250		not see thy Hand.
	Prince	These Lyes are like the [3] Father that begets them, grosse as a Mountaine, open, palpable. Why thou Clay-brayn'd Guts, thou Knotty-pated Foole, thou Horson ob-
255		scene greasie Tallow Catch.
	Falstaffe	What, art thou mad? art thou mad? is not the truth, the truth?
	Prince	Why, how could'st thou know these men in Kendall Greene, when it was so darke, thou could'st not
260		see thy Hand? Come, tell us your reason: what say'st thou to this?
	Poines	Come, your reason Jack, your reason.

L 57 - a (or j) / R 57 - a (or j) : 2. 4. 207 - 235

[A][1] most modern texts suggest the next six speeches of Falstaffe's listeners (five for the Prince and one for Poines) are spoken as asides

[▼][2] Q1 = their, Q2 - 5/Ff = 'his'

[▼][3] Q1/F4 = 'their', Q2 - 5/F1 - 3 = 'the'

Falstaffe	What, upon compulsion?
265		No : were [1] I at the Strappado, or all the Racks in the World, I would not tell you on compulsion.
	Give you a reason on compulsi- on?
270		If Reasons were as plentie [2] as Blacke-berries, I would give no man a Reason upon compulsion, I.
Prince	Ile be no longer guiltie of this sinne.
	This san- guine Coward, this Bed-presser, this Hors-back-breaker,
275		this huge Hill of Flesh.
Falstaffe	Away [3] you Starveling, you Elfe-skin, [4] you dried Neats tongue, Bulles-pissell, you stocke-fish : O for breth to utter. [5]
	What is like thee?
280		You Tailors yard, you sheath you Bow-case, you vile standing tucke.
Prince	Well, breath a-while, and then °to't againe : and when thou hast tyr'd thy selfe in base comparisons, heare me speake but thus. [6]
285	**Poines**	Marke Jacke.
Prince	We two, saw you foure set on foure and bound them, and were Masters of their Wealth : mark now how a plaine Tale shall put you downe.
	Then did we two, set
290		on you foure, and with a word, outfac'd you from your prize, and have it : yea, and can shew it you [7] in the House.
	And Falstaffe, you caried your Guts away as nimbly, with as quicke dexteritie, and roared for mercy, and still ranne [8] and roar'd, as ever I heard Bull-Calfe.

[O][1] most modern texts follow Qq and set the oath 'Zoundes, and I were', Ff = 'No: were I'

[W][2] Q1 = 'plentifull', Q2 - 5/Ff = 'plentie'

[O][3] most modern texts follow Qq and set the oath 'Zbloud', Ff = 'Away'

[W][4] though some modern texts agree with Qq/Ff and print this as 'Elfe-skin', one gloss = 'eel-skin'

[PCT][5] most modern texts follow Qq's lighter or lack of punctuation here, and usually replace Ff's period with a comma, thus allowing the sentence to flow, rather than heightening Falstaffe's sense of bluster within the period

[W][6] Q1 - 3 = 'this', Q4 - 5/Ff = 'thus'

[W][7] most modern texts follow Qq and set 'here', omitted by Ff

[W][8] Qq = 'run', Ff = 'ranne'

295   What a Slave art
thou, to hacke thy sword as thou hast done, and then say
it was in fight.
                     What trick? what device? what starting
hole canst thou now find out, to hide thee from this open
300   and apparant shame?

Poines   Come, let's heareJacke :   What tricke hast
thou now?

Falstaffe   [1] I knew ye as well as he that made ye.
                                   Why heare
305   •ye my Masters, was it for me to kill the Heire apparant?
Should I turne upon the true Prince?
                             Why, thou knowest
I am as valiant as Hercules :   but beware Instinct, the Lion
will not touch the true Prince :   Instinct is a great matter.
310   I was [2] a Coward on Instinct :   I shall thinke the better of
my selfe, and thee, during my life :   I, for a valiant Lion,
and thou for a true Prince.
                          But [3] Lads, I am glad you have
the Mony.
315   Hostesse, clap to the doores :   watch tonight,
pray to morrow.
                  Gallants, Lads, Boyes, Harts of Gold,
all the good Titles of [4] Fellowship come to you.
                                   What,
320   shall we be merry? shall we have a Play extempory.

Prince   Content, and the argument shall be, thy runing
away.

Falstaffe   A, no more of that Hall, and thou lovest me.

ENTER HOSTESSE

Hostesse   My Lord, the Prince ?   R 57 - a (or j)

325 **Prince**   How now my Lady the Hostesse, what say'st
thou to me?

Hostesse   Marry, my Lord, there is a Noble man of the
Court at doore would speake with you :   hee sayes, hee
comes from your Father.

O [1]   most modern texts follow Qq and set the oath omitted by Ff, 'By the Lord,'

W [2]   most modern texts follow Q1 and set 'now', omitted by Q2 - 5/Ff

O [3]   most modern texts follow Qq and set the oath omitted by Ff, 'by the Lord'

W [4]   Qq and most modern texts = 'titles of good fellowship', Ff = 'good Titles of Fellowship'

330	**Prince**	Give him as much as will make him a Royall man, and send him backe againe to my Mother.
	Falstaffe	What manner of man is hee?
	Hostesse	An old man.
	Falstaffe	What doth Gravitie out of his Bed at Midnight?
335		Shall I give him his answere?
	Prince	Prethee doe Jacke.
	Falstaffe	'Faith, and Ile send him packing.

[Exit]

	Prince	Now Sirs : [1] you fought faire ; so did you Peto, so did you Bardol : you are Lyons too, you ranne
340		away upon instinct : you will not touch the true Prince ; no, fie.
	Bardolph	'Faith, I ranne when I saw others runne.
	Prince	[2] Tell mee now in earnest, how came Falstaffes Sword so hackt?
345	**Peto**	Why, he hackt it with his Dagger, and said, hee would sweare truth out of England, but hee would make you beleeve it was done in fight, and perswaded us to doe the like.
	Bardolph	Yea, and to tickle our Noses with Spear-grasse,
350		to make them bleed, and then to beslubber our garments with it, and sweare it was the blood of true men. I did that I did not this seven yeeres [3] before, I blusht to heare his monstrous devices.
355	**Prince**	O Villaine, thou stolest a Cup of Sacke eigh- teene yeeres agoe, and wert taken with the manner, and ever since thou hast blusht extempore : thou hadst fire and sword on thy side, and yet thou ranst away ; what instinct hadst thou for it?
360	**Bardolph**	My Lord, doe you see these Meteors? doe you behold these Exhalations?

L 58 - a (or j) : 2. 4. 290 - 320

o 1 most modern texts follow Qq and set the oath omitted by Ff, 'birlady', i.e. 'by our lady'

o 2 most modern texts follow Qq and set 'Faith', which is omitted by Ff

w 3 Q1 - 3 = 'yeare', Q4 - 5/Ff = 'yeeres'

	Prince	I doe.
	Bardolph	What thinke you they portend?
	Prince	Hot Livers, and cold Purses.
365	**Bardolph**	Choler, my Lord, if rightly taken.
	Prince	No, if rightly taken, Halter.

ENTER FALSTAFFE

Heere comes leaneJacke, heere comes bare-bone. How
now my sweet Creature of Bombast, how long is't agoe,
370   Jacke, since thou saw'st thine owne Knee?

Falstaffe   My owne Knee?
When I was about thy yeeres
(Hal) I was not an Eagles Talent in the Waste, I could
have crept into any Aldermans Thumbe-Ring :   a plague
375   of sighing and griefe, it blowes a man up like a Bladder.

There's villanous Newes abroad :   heere was SirJohn
Braby [1] from your Father ;   you must goe [2] to the Court in
the Morning.
The [3] same mad fellow of the North, Percy ;
380   and hee of Wales, that gave Amamon the Bastinado,
and made Lucifer Cuckold, and swore-the Devill his true
Liege-man upon the Crosse of a Welch-hooke ;   what a
plague call you him?

Poines   O, Glendower.

385   **Falstaffe**   Owen, Owen ;   the same, and his Sonne in Law
Mortimer, and old Northumberland, and the [4] sprightly
Scot of Scots, Dowglas, that runnes a Horse-backe up a
Hill perpendicular.

Prince   Hee that rides at high speede, and with a [5] Pistoll
390   kills a Sparrow flying.

Falstaffe   You have hit it.   L 58 - a (or j)

L 58 - a (or j) : 2. 4. 321 - 347

[N][1] Q1 - 3 = 'Bracy', Q4 - 5/Ff = 'Braby', (there is no known historical figure who corresponds to this character)
[▼][2] most modern texts follow Q1 - 4 and omit 'goe', which is set by Q5/Ff
[▼][3] Q1 - 4 = 'That', Q5/Ff = 'The'
[▼][4] Q1 - 2 = 'that', Q3 - 5/Ff = 'the'
[▼][5] Q1 - 2 = 'his', Q3 - 5 = 'a'

	Prince	So did he never the Sparrow.
	Falstaffe	Well, that Rascall hath good mettall in him, hee will not runne.
395	**Prince**	Why, what a Rascall art thou then, to prayse him so for running?
	Falstaffe	A Horse-backe (ye Cuckoe) but a foot [1] hee will not budge a foot.
	Prince	Yes Jacke, upon instinct.
400	**Falstaffe**	I grant ye, upon instinct: Well, hee is there too, and one Mordake, and a thousand blew-Cappes more.

Worcester is stolne away by Night: [2] thy Fathers Beard is turn'd white with the Newes; you may buy Land now as cheape as stinking Mackrell.

405	**Prince**	[3] Then "tis like, if there come a hot Sunne,[4] and this civill buffetting hold, wee shall buy Maiden-heads as they buy Hob-nayles, by the Hundreds.

	Falstaffe	By the Masse Lad, thou say'st true, it is like wee shall have good trading that way.
410		But tell me Hal, art not thou horrible afear'd? thou being Heire apparant, could the World picke thee out three such Enemyes a-gaine, as that Fiend Dowglas, that Spirit Percy, and that Devill Glendower?
415		Art not thou [5] horrible afraid?
		Doth not thy blood thrill at it?

	Prince	Not a whit: [6] I lacke some of thy instinct.
	Falstaffe	Well, thou wilt be horrible chidde to morrow,
420		when thou commest to thy Father: if thou doe [7] love me, practise an answere.

---

[1] Q1/4 - 5/Ff = 'a foot', most modern texts follow Q2-3 and set 'afoot', thus maintaining the elegant pun

[2] Q1 - 4 = 'to night', Q5/Ff = 'by Night'

[3] most modern texts follow Q1 - 2 and set 'Why', omitted by Q3 - 5/Ff

[4] Q1 - 3 = 'June', Q4 - 5/Ff = 'Sunne'

[5] Q1 - 2 'thou not', Q3 - 5/Ff = 'not thou'

[6] Qq/most modern texts set the oath 'ifaith': Ff omit the word

[7] most modern texts follow Q3 - 5/Ff and set 'doe', omitted by Q1 - 2

Prince Doe thou stand for my Father, and examine mee
upon the particulars of my Life.

Falstaffe Shall I? content: This Chayre shall bee my
State, this Dagger my Scepter, and this Cushion my
Crowne.

Prince Thy State is taken for a Joyn'd-Stoole, thy Golden Scepter for a Leaden Dagger, and thy precious rich
Crowne, for a pittifull bald Crowne.

Falstaffe Well, and the fire of Grace be not quite out of
thee, now shalt thou be moved.
Give me a Cup of Sacke
to make *mine eyes looke redde, that it may be thought I
have wept, for I must speake in passion, and I will doe it
in King Cambyses vaine.

Prince Well, heere is my Legge.

Falstaffe And heere is my speech: stand aside Nobilitie.

Hostesse [1] This is excellent sport, yfaith.

Falstaffe Weepe not, sweet Queene, for trickling teares
are vaine.

Hostesse O the Father, how hee holdes his countenance?

Falstaffe For Gods sake Lords, convey my trustfull [2] Queen,
For teares doe stop the floud-gates of her eyes. [3]

Hostesse O rare,[4] he doth it as like one of these harlotry
Players, as ever I see.

Falstaffe Peace good Pint-pot, peace good Tickle-braine.

Harry, I doe not onely marvell where thou spendest thy
time; but also, how thou art accompanied: For though
the Camomile, the more it is troden,[5] the faster it growes;
yet Youth, the more it is wasted, the sooner it weares.

R 58 - a (or j) : 2. 4. 376 - 402

O [1] most modern texts follow Qq and set the oath omitted by Ff, 'O Jesu,'

W [2] though most modern texts agree with Qq/Ff and print this as 'trustfull', one gloss = 'tristfull', probably a dig at the Hostesse's profession - (presumably she is named 'Mistresse Quicklie' for a reason)

VP [3] as set in Q1/F1 - 3 both this speech and the first line of his next could be in verse, a delightful idea if at first Falstaffe is thoroughly enjoying/overdoing his kingly role: F4/most modern texts set these lines as prose

O [4] most modern texts follow Qq and set the oath 'O Jesu,': Ff = 'O rare'

W [5] most modern texts follow Q1 - 4 and set 'on', omitted by Q5/Ff

[1] Thou art my Sonne: I have partly thy Mothers Word,
partly my [2] Opinion; but chiefely, a villanous tricke of
thine Eye, and a foolish hanging of thy nether Lippe, that
455   doth warrant me.
                If then thou be Sonne to mee, heere
lyeth [3] the point: why, being Sonne to me, art thou so
poynted at?
            Shall the blessed Sonne [4] of Heaven prove a
460   Micher, and eate Black-berryes? a question not to bee
askt.
         Shall the Sonne of England prove a Theefe, and
take Purses? a question to be askt.
                    There is a thing,
465   Harry, which thou hast often heard of, and it is knowne to   R 58 - a (or j)
many in our Land, by the Name of Pitch: this Pitch (as
ancient Writers doe report) doth defile; so doth the companie thou keepest: for Harry, now I doe not speake to
thee in Drinke, but in Teares; not in Pleasure, but in Pas-
470   sion; not in Words onely, but in Woes also: and yet
there is a vertuous man, whom I have often noted in thy
companie, but I know not his Name.

Prince   What manner of man, and it like your Majestie?

475 **Falstaffe**   A goodly portly man yfaith, and a corpulent,
of a chearefull Looke, a pleasing Eye, and a most noble
Carriage, and as I thinke, his age some fiftie, or (byrlady)
inclining to threescore; and now I remember mee, his
Name is Falstaffe: if that man should be lewdly given,
480   hee deceives [5] mee; for Harry, I see Vertue in his Lookes.

    If then the Tree may be knowne by the Fruit, as the Fruit
by the Tree, then peremptorily I speake it, there is Vertue
in that Falstaffe: him keepe with, the rest banish.
                         And
485   tell mee now, thou naughtie Varlet, tell mee, where hast
thou beene this moneth?

Prince   Do'st thou speake like a King? doe thou stand
for mee, and Ile play my Father.

---

[w][1] most modern texts follow Q1 - 2 and set 'That', omitted by Q3 - 5/Ff

[w][2] most modern texts follow Q1 - 2 and set 'owne', omitted by Q3 - 5/Ff

[w][3] Q1 - 2- = 'lies', Q3 - 5/Ff = 'lyeth'

[w][4] Q2 - 5/Ff = 'Sonne', most modern texts follow Q1 and set 'sunne', thus preserving the pun

[w][5] Q1 - 2 = 'deceiveth', Q3 - 5/Ff = 'deceives'

	Falstaffe	Depose me : if thou do'st it halfe so gravely, so
490		majestically, both in word and matter, hang me up by the
		heeles for a Rabbet-sucker, or a Poulters Hare.
	Prince	Well, heere I am set. [1]
	Falstaffe	And heere I stand : judge my Masters.
	Prince	Now Harry, whence come you?
495	**Falstaffe**	My Noble Lord, from East-cheape.
	Prince	The complaints I heare of thee, are grievous.
	Falstaffe	Yfaith,[2] my Lord, they are false : Nay, Ile tickle
		ye for a young prince.
	Prince	Swearest thou, ungracious Boy? henceforth
500		ne're looke on me : thou art violently carryed away from
		Grace : there is a Devill haunts thee, in the likenesse of a
		fat old [3] Man ; a Tunne of Man is thy Companion : Why
		do'st thou converse with that Trunke of Humors, that
		Boulting-Hutch of Beastlinesse, that swolne Parcell of
505		Dropsies, that huge Bombard of Sacke, that stuft Cloake-
		bagge of Guts, that rosted Manning Tree†[4] Oxe with the
		Pudding in his Belly, that reverend Vice, that grey Ini-
		quitie, that Father Ruffian, that Vanitie in yeeres? where-
		in is he good, but to taste Sacke, and drinke it? wherein
510		neat and cleanly, but to carve a Capon, and eat it? where-
		in Cunning, but in Craft? where in Craftie, but in Villa-
		nie? wherein Villanous, but in all things? wherein wor-
		thy, but in nothing?
	Falstaffe	I would your Grace would take me with you :
515		whom meanes your Grace?
	Prince	That villanous abhominable mis-leader of
		Youth, Falstaffe, that old white-bearded Sathan.
	Falstaffe	My Lord, the man I know.
	Prince	I know thou do'st.
520	**Falstaffe**	But to say, I know more harme in him then in
		my selfe, were to say more then I know.

L 59 - a (or j) : 2. 4. 435 - 467

SD[1] most modern texts explain that Falstaffe is now standing and the Prince has taken the 'throne'

O[2] most modern texts follow Qq and set the oath omitted by Ff, ', Zbloud', and add 'I faith' to the end of the speech

W[3] Q1 - 4 = 'an old fat', Q5/Ff = 'a fat old'

W[4] F1 = 'T ree', F2 = 'Tree'

That hee is olde
(the more the pittie) his white hayres doe witnesse it:
but that hee is (saving your reverence) a Whore-ma-
525   ster, that I utterly deny.

          If Sacke and Sugar bee a fault,
*Heaven helpe the Wicked: if to be olde and merry, be a
sinne, then many an olde Hoste that I know, is damn'd:
if to be fat, be to be hated, then Pharaohs leane Kine are
530   to be loved.

          No, my good Lord, banish Peto, banish
Bardolph, banish Poines: but for sweete Jacke Falstaffe,
kinde Jacke Falstaffe, true Jacke Falstaffe, valiant Jacke Falstaffe, and therefore more valiant, being as hee is olde Jack

535   Falstaffe,° banish not him thy Harryes companie,° banish   L 59 - a (or j)
not him thy Harryes companie; ° banish plumpe Jacke, and
banish all the World. ° 1

| Prince | I doe, I will. 2 |

ENTER BARDOLPH RUNNING

| Bardolph | O, my Lord, my Lord, the Sherife, with a most |
540 | | most 3 monstrous Watch, is at the doore. |

| Falstaffe | Out *you Rogue, play out the Play: I have much |
| | to say in the behalfe of that Falstaffe. |

ENTER THE HOSTESSE

| Hostesse | O 4, my Lord, my Lord. |

| Falstaffe | 5 Heigh, heigh, the Devill rides upon a Fiddle- |
545 | | sticke: what's the matter? |

Hostesse	The Sherife and all the Watch are at the
	doore: they are come to search the House, shall I let
	them in?

VP 1
  though Qq/Ff set the ending of the speech as prose, at least one modern text suggests setting Falstaffe's final
SD 'plea' in verse (a style he hardly ever uses)
2
  in view of the two forthcoming entrances from characters who have been on stage throughout this scene
(Bardolph and the Hostesse) most modern texts add two stage directions, the first for knocking to come from
offstage, the second for Bardolph and the Hostesse (and sometimes Francis) to exit
W 3
  most modern texts follow Qq/F2 and omit the second 'most' as set by F1
O 4
  most modern texts follow Qq and set the oath omitted by Ff, 'Jesu,'
P 5
  perhaps because of the outburst just erupted from Falstaffe, most modern texts follow Q1 - 3 and assign this
speech to the Prince (whereas Q4 - 5/Ff have given it to Falstaffe)

Falstaffe	Do'st thou heare Hal, never call a true peece of	
550		Gold a Counterfeit: thou art essentially made,[1] without
		seeming so.
Prince	And thou a naturall Coward, without in-	
		stinct.
Falstaffe	I deny your Maior: if you will deny the	
555		Sherife, so: if not, let him enter.

                                           If I become not a Cart

		as well as another man, a plague on my bringing up: I
		hope I shall as soone be strangled with a Halter, as ano-
		ther.
560	**Prince**	Goe hide thee behinde the Arras, the rest
		walke up above.

                                Now my Masters, for a true Face and

		good Conscience.
	Falstaffe	Both which I have had: but their date is out,
565		and therefore Ile hide me.

[Exit] [2]

Prince	Call in the Sherife.	

ENTER SHERIFE AND THE CARRIER

Prince	Now Master Sherife, what is your will with	
	mee? °	
Sherife	First pardon me, my Lord.	
570		A Hue and Cry° hath
	followed certaine men unto this house. °	
Prince	What men? °	
Sherife	One of them is well knowne, my gracious Lord,°	
	a grosse fat man.	
575	**Carrier**	As fat as Butter. ° [3]

R 59 - a (or j) : 2. 4. 491 - 511

W [1]   Qq/F1 - 2 = 'made', F3-4 and some modern texts = 'mad'

SD [2]   because of a later line from the Prince (line 592, next page) some modern texts suggest Falstaffe hides himself behind the Arras

VP [3]   though Qq/Ff set the passage in prose, most modern texts set it in verse as shown: however, this removes the moment when the Prince feels it necessary to move into verse to deal with the Sherife: (it would seem the Qq/Ff verse demonstrates how he asserts his authority, viz. with quiet and graceful argument)

Prince	The man, I doe assure you, is not heere,	
	For I my selfe at this time have imploy'd him:	
	And Sherife, I will engage my word to thee,	
	That I will by to morrow Dinner time,	
580	Send him to answere thee, or any man,	
	For anything he shall be charg'd withall:	
	And so let me entreat you, leave the house.	
Sherife	I will, my Lord: there are two Gentlemen	
	Have in this Robberie lost three hundred Markes.	
585 **Prince**	It may be so: if he have robb'd these men,	
	He shall be answerable: and so farewell.	
Sherife	Good Night, my Noble Lord.	
Prince	I thinke it is good Morrow, is it not?	
Sherife	Indeede, my Lord, I thinke it be two a Clocke.	

[Exit]

590 **Prince**	This oyly Rascall is knowne as well as Poules: °	
	goe call him forth. ° 1	
Peto 2	Falstaffe? fast asleepe behinde the Arras, and	
	snorting like a Horse.	
Prince	Harke, how hard he fetches breath: search his	
595	Pockets.	R 59 - a (or j)

**HE SEARCHETH HIS POCKETS, AND FINDETH
CERTAINE PAPERS**

Prince	What hast thou found?
Peto	Nothing but Papers, my Lord.
Prince	Let's see, what be they? 3 reade them.
Peto	Item, a Capon. ii. s. ii. d. 4
600	Item, Sawce. iiii. d.
	Item, Sacke, two Gallons. v. s. viii. d.

VP 1   though most modern texts follow Qq/Ff and set this in prose, at least one text suggests the speech should be verse

P 2   though Qq/Ff set the prefix for Peto throughout the remainder of the scene, some commentators suggest the
character could be Harvey, others the Prince's chief crony, Poines

W 3   Q1 - 3 = 'see what they be', Q4 - 5 = 'see what be they', Ff = 'see, what be they?'

AB 4   in all the following amounts, the 's' stands for shillings and the 'd' for pence

Item, Anchoves and Sacke after Supper. ii. s. vi. d.

Item, Bread ob. [1]

Prince   O monstrous, but one halfepenny-worth of
605   Bread to this intollerable deale of Sacke?

                                                  What there is
                    else, keepe close, wee'le read it at more advantage: there
                    let him sleepe till day.

                                        Ile to the Court in the Morning:
610   Wee must all to the Warres, and thy place shall be hono-
                    rable.

                                        Ile procure this fat Rogue a Charge of Foot,
                    and I know his death will be a Match [2] of Twelve-score.

                    The Money shall be pay'd backe againe with advantage.

615   Be with me betimes in the Morning: and so good mor-
                    row Peto.

Peto   Good morrow, good my Lord.

                              [Exeunt]

AB [1] 'ob' stands for a half of one penny (a halfpenny)

W [2] Q1 - 3/F3 and most modern texts = 'march', Q4 - 5/F1 - 2 = 'Match'

57

Actus Tertius.   Scena Prima

ENTER HOTSPURRE, WORCESTER, LORD MORTIMER,
OWEN GLENDOWER [1]

Mortimer	These promises are faire, the parties sure, And our induction full of prosperous hope.
Hotspurre	Lord Mortimer, and Cousin Glendower, Will you sit downe? [2]

5
	And Unckle Worcester; a plague upon it, I have forgot the Mappe.
Glendower	No, here it is: Sit Cousin Percy, sit good Cousin Hotspurre: For by that Name, as oft as Lancaster doth speake of you,

10
His Cheekes looke [3] pale, and with a rising sigh,
He wisheth you in Heaven. [4]

Hotspurre	And you in Hell,° as oft as he heares Owen Glen- dower spoke of. °
Glendower	I cannot blame him: At my Nativitie,

15
The front of Heaven was full of fierie shapes,
Of burning Cressets: and at my Birth,
The frame and [5] foundation of the Earth
Shak'd like a Coward.

Hotspurre	Why so it would have done° at the same season,

20
if your Mothers Cat° had but kitten'd, though your selfe
had never been borne. ° [6]

Glendower	I say the Earth did shake when I was borne.

L 60 - a (or j) : 3. 1. 1 - 20

[SD 1] because of the ensuing dialogue, most modern texts suggest one of them or an Attendant has a map

[SD 2] most modern texts suggest all sit but Hotspurre, who finally seats himself in four lines time

[W 3] Qq and most modern texts = 'cheek lookes', Ff = 'Cheekes looke'

[VP 4] though Qq set this opening passage as prose, most modern texts follow Ff and set it as verse, and even change Ff's prose of Hotspurre's next speech into verse, as shown

[W 5] most modern texts follow Q1 and set 'huge', omitted by Q2 - 5/Ff

[VP 6] this is the second time that Qq/Ff's prose setting for a Hotspurre insult to Glendower has been changed to verse by the modern texts: however, the original setting offers splendid theatrical possibilities, as if (perhaps) Hotspurre is not yet giving them public weight or fully formal utterance

Hotspurre	'	And I say the Earth was not of my minde,
		If you suppose, as fearing you, it shooke.

25   **Glendower**   The Heavens were all on fire, the Earth did
tremble.

Hotspurre   Oh, then the Earth shooke→ [1]
To see the Heavens on fire,
And not in feare of your Nativitie.

30   Diseased Nature oftentimes breakes forth
In strange eruptions; and [2] the teeming Earth
Is with a kinde of Collick pincht and vext,
By the imprisoning of unruly Winde
Within her Wombe: which for enlargement striving,
35   Shakes the old Beldame Earth, and tombles [3] downe   L 60 - a (or j)
Steeples, and mosse-growne Towers.
                 At your Birth,
Our Grandam Earth, having this distemperature,
In passion shooke.

40   **Glendower**   Cousin: of many men
I doe not beare these Crossings: Give me leave
To tell you once againe, that at my Birth
The front of Heaven was full of fierie shapes,
The Goates ranne from the Mountaines, and the Heards
45   Were strangely clamorous to the frighted fields:
These signes have markt me extraordinarie,
And all the courses of my Life doe shew,
I am not in the Roll of common men.

Where is the[4] Living, clipt in with the Sea,
50   That chides the Bankes of England, Scotland, and [5] Wales,
Which calls me Pupill, or hath read to me?

And bring him out, that is but Womans Sonne,
Can trace me in the tedious wayes of Art,
And hold me pace in deepe experiments.

L 60 - a (or j) / R 60 - a (or j) : 3. 1. 21 - 48

SP [1]
most modern texts follow Qq and set these two short Ff lines as one split verse line: however, the 'peculiar'
Ff setting comes at the beginning of yet another Hotspurre to Glendower 'insult' speech, which may explain why
the line (yet again) is not set in 'correct' fully formalised verse

W [2]
Q1 - 3 = 'oft', Q4 = 'of', Q5/Ff = 'and'

W [3]
Q1 - 4 = 'topples', Q5 = 'toples', F1 - 2 = 'tombles', F3 - 4 = 'tumbles'

W [4]
Q1 - 3 and most modern texts = 'he', Q4 - 5/Ff = 'the'

W [5]
most modern texts follow Q1 - 4 and omit 'and', which is set by Q5/Ff

55	Hotspurre	I thinke there's¹ no man speakes better Welsh : Ile to Dinner.
	Mortimer	Peace Cousin Percy, you will make him mad.
	Glendower	I can call Spirits from the vastie Deepe.
60	Hotspurre	Why so can I, or so can any man : But will they come, when you doe call for them?
	Glendower	Why, I can teach *thee, Cousin, to command the Devill.
65	Hotspurre	And I can teach thee, Cousin,² to shame the Devill, By telling truth. *Tell truth, and shame the Devill.* If thou have power to rayse him, bring him hither, And Ile be sworne, I have power to shame him hence. Or, while you live, tell truth, and shame the Devill.
70	Mortimer	Come, come, no more of this unprofitable Chat.
	Glendower	Three times hath Henry Bullingbrooke made head Against my Power : thrice from the Banks of Wye, And sandy-bottom'd Severne, have I hent³ him Bootlesse home, and Weather-beaten backe.
75	Hotspurre	Home without Bootes, → ⁴ And in foule Weather too, How scapes he Agues in the Devils name?
80	Glendower	Come, heere's the Mappe : → Shall wee divide our Right, According to our three-fold order ta'ne?
	Mortimer	The Arch-Deacon hath divided it Into three Limits, very equally : England, from Trent, and Severne hitherto, By South and East, is to my part assign'd :

ᵂ₁ since Qq/Ff set a nine syllable line, some modern texts set 'there is' for Qq/Ff's 'there's': however, one text
suggests setting 'speaketh' instead of 'speakes', and that Hotspurre gets to his feet

ᵂ₂ Q1 - 4 = 'coose', Q5 = 'coosen', Ff = 'Cousin'

ᵂ₃ Q1 - 3/F3 = 'sent', Q4 - 5/F1 - 2 = 'hent'

ˢᴾ₄ again at the start of another Hotspurre - Glendower insult Ff show a split line: Qq and most modern texts set
the two short lines as one line of split verse: the same restructuring applies to the first such split line for
Glendower in the speech immediately following: in both cases it would seem that the Ff setting clearly
delineates the almost loss of control that both men are undergoing in their mutual rivalry

85		All Westward, Wales, beyond the Severne shore,
		And all the fertile Land within that bound,
		To Owen Glendower: And deare Couze, to you
		The remnant Northward, lying off from Trent.
		And out Indentures Tripartite are drawne:
90		Which being sealed enterchangeably,
		(A Businesse that this Night may execute)
		To morrow, Cousin Percy, you and I,
		And my good Lord of Worcester, will set forth,
		To meete your Father, and the Scottish Power,
95		As is appointed us at Shrewsbury.
		My Father Glendower is not readie yet,
		Nor shall wee neede his helpe these fourteene dayes:
	[1]	Within that space, you may have drawne together
		Your Tenants, Friends, and neighbouring Gentlemen.

100	**Glendower**	A shorter time shall send me to you, Lords:	
		And in my Conduct shall your Ladies come,	
		From whom you now must steale, and take no leave,	
		For there will be a World of Water shed,	R 60 - a (or j)
		Upon the parting of your Wives and you.	

105	**Hotspurre**	Me thinks my Moity, North from Burton here,
		In quantitie equals not one of yours:
		See, how this River comes me cranking in,
		And cuts me from the best of all my Land,
		A huge halfe Moone, a monstrous Cantle out.
110		Ile have the Currant in this place damn'd [2] up,
		And here the smug and Silver Trent shall runne,
		In a new Channell, faire and evenly:
		It shall not winde with such a deepe indent,
		To rob me of so rich a Bottome here.

115	**Glendower**	Not winde? it shall, it must, you see it doth.

Mortimer	Yea,° but marke how he beares his course,
	And runnes me up,° with like advantage on the other side,° [3]

	Gelding the opposed Continents as much,
	As on the other side it takes from you.

R 60 - a (or j) / L 61 - a (or j) : 3. 1. 75 - 110

WHO [1]
  some modern texts explain this is spoken to Glendower

W [2]
  most modern texts follow Q3 - 5 = 'damd', Q1-2/Ff = 'damn'd'

VP/LS [3]
  Qq set this whole speech in prose, Ff in verse as shown: most modern texts keep the verse but restructure the first two lines rather peculiarly (1/11/10 syllables) thus normalising Mortimer's remarks - after a delay before starting to reply; the Ff irregularity (8/14 syllables) allows for a slow burn, with Mortimer exploding on the second line, and then recovering from the rest of the speech

120	**Worcester**	Yea, but a little Charge will trench him here, And on this North side winne this Cape of Land, And then he runnes straight and even.
	Hotspurre	Ile have it so, a little Charge will doe it.
	Glendower	Ile not have it alter'd.
125	**Hotspurre**	Will not you?
	Glendower	No, nor you shall not.
	Hotspurre	Who shall say me nay?
	Glendower	Why, that will I. [1]
130	**Hotspurre**	Let me not understand you then, speake it in Welsh.
	Glendower	I can speake English, Lord, as well as you : For I was trayn'd up in the English Court; Where, being but young, I framed to the Harpe
135		Many an English Dittie, lovely well, And gave the Tongue a helpefull Ornament; A Vertue that was never seene in you.
	Hotspurre	Marry, and I am glad of it with all my heart, I had rather be a Kitten, and cry mew, Then one of these same Meeter Ballad-mongers :
140		I had rather heare a Brazen Candlestick [2] turn'd, Or a dry Wheele grate on the Axle-tree, And that would set my teeth nothing an [3] edge, Nothing so much, as mincing Poetrie; 'Tis like the forc't gate of a shuffling Nagge.
145	**Glendower**	Come, you shall have Trent turn'd.
	Hotspurre	I doe not care : Ile give thrice so much Land To any well-deserving friend; But in the way of Bargaine, marke ye me, Ile cavill on the ninth part of a hayre.
150		Are the Indentures drawne? shall we be gone?

L 61 - a (or j) : 3. 1. 111 - 139

[SP] [1] the actor has choice as to which two of these five short lines may be joined as two lines of split verse: probably the best pairing would be #1 + #2, #3 + #4, followed immediately by #5, and then a pause before Hotspurre utters yet another insult

▼ [2] Q1 - 3 = 'cansticke', Q4 - 5/Ff = 'Candlestick'

▼ [3] Q3-4 and most modern texts = 'on', Q1 - 3/Ff = 'an'

62

Glendower	The Moone shines faire, → [1]	
	You may away by Night:	
	Ile haste the Writer; and withall,	
	Breake with your Wives, of your departure hence:	
155	I am afraid my Daughter will runne madde,	
	So much she doteth on her Mortimer.	

[Exit]

Mortimer	Fie, Cousin Percy, how you crosse my Fa-	
	ther.	
Hotspurre	I cannot chuse: sometime he angers me,	
160	With telling me of the Moldwarpe and the Ant,	
	Of the Dreamer Merlin, and his Prophecies;	
	And of a Dragon, and a finne-lesse Fish,	
	A clip-wing'd Griffin, and a moulten Raven,	
	A couching Lyon, and a rampling Cat,	
165	And such a deale of skimble-skamble Stuffe,	
	As puts me from my Faith.	
	I tell you what,	
	He held me [2] last Night, at least, nine howres,	
	In reckning up the severall Devils Names,	
170	That were his Lacqueyes: → [3]	L 61 - a (or j)
	I cry'd hum, and well, goe too,	
	But mark'd him not a word.	
	O, *he is as tedious	
	As a tyred Horse, a rayling Wife,	
175	Worse then a smoakie House.	
	*I had rather live	
	With Cheese and Garlick in a Windmill farre,	
	Then feede on Cates, and have him talke to me,	
	In any Summer-House in Christendome.	
180	**Mortimer** In faith he was [4] a worthy Gentleman,	
	Exceeding [5] well read, and profited,	

> In strange Concealements:
> Valiant as a Lyon,° and wondrous affable,
> And as bountifull,° as Mynes of India.

L 61 - a (or j) / R 61 - a (or j) :   3. 1. 140 - 167

[SP] [1]
again the Ff only split line is theatrically very useful, since it allows Glendower a moment of pause before makes his mind fully known: most modern texts follow Qq and set the two short lines as one split verse line, thus regularising the potentially highly dramatic moment

[W] [2]
to create a ten syllable line some modern texts add 'up' or 'the' or 'but', none of which is set by Qq/Ff

[SP] [3]
most modern texts follow Qq and turn these two short F1 lines into one split verse line, which yet again robs Hotspurre of any choked-off reaction as he describes what to him is Glendower's outlandishness

[W] [4]
most modern texts follow Q1 - 2 and set 'is', Q3 - 5/Ff = 'was'

[W] [5]
Q1 - 2 = 'Exceedingly', Q3 - 5/Ff = 'Exceeding'

185		Shall I tell you, Cousin,° ¹

He holds your temper in a high respect,
And curbs himselfe, even of his naturall scope,
When you doe crosse ² his humor :   faith he does.

I warrant you, that man is not alive,
190   Might so have tempted him, as you have done,
Without the taste of danger, and reproofe :
But doe not use it oft, let me entreat you.

Worcester   In faith, my Lord, you are too wilfull blame,
And since your comming hither, have done enough,
195   To put him quite besides his patience.

You must needes learne, Lord, to amend this fault :
Though sometimes it shew Greatnesse, Courage, Blood,
And that's the dearest grace it renders you ;
Yet oftentimes it doth present harsh Rage,
200   Defect of manners, want of Government,
Pride, Haughtinesse, Opinion, and Disdaine :
The least of which, haunting a Nobleman,
Loseth mens hearts, and leaves behinde a stayne
Upon the beautie of all parts besides,
205   Beguiling them of commendation.
                                    }

Hotspurre   Well, I am school'd : → ³
Good-manners be your speede ;
Heere come your ⁴ Wives, and let us take our leave.

ENTER GLENDOWER, WITH THE LADIES ⁵

Mortimer   This is the deadly spight, that angers me,
210   My Wife can speake no English, I no Welsh.

Glendower   My Daugher weepes, ˙shee'le not part with you,
Shee'le be a Souldier too, shee'le to the Warres.

Mortimer   Good Father tell her, that she and my Aunt Percy
Shall follow in your Conduct speedily.

LS ¹ Ff allow for Mortimer's awkward pauses ((5/12-13/10-11/6 syllables) as he sings his father-in-law's praises:
the Qq/modern texts' forced regularity (11-12/11/11-12) creates bluster instead

W ² Qq most modern texts = 'come crosse', Ff = 'doe crosse'

SP ³ most modern texts follow Qq and turn these two short Ff lines into one split verse line, though this seems to
rob Hotspurre of his (perhaps deliberate) tantalising of his Uncle Worcester and Mortimer before reply

W ⁴ Q1 - 2 and most modern texts = 'come our', Q3 - 5/Ff = 'come your'

SD ⁵ because of the ensuing dialogue, some modern texts suggest Mortimer's wife weeps and speaks to him in
Welsh now (though Qq/Ff set three later directions for her to do so) and weeps

**GLENDOWER SPEAKES TO HER IN WELSH, AND SHE AN-
SWERS HIM IN THE SAME**

215	Glendower	Shee is desperate heere:
		A peevish selfe-will'd Harlotry,
		One that no perswasion can doe good upon. [1]

THE LADY SPEAKES IN WELSH

	Mortimer	I understand thy Lookes: thy pretty Welsh
		Which thou powr'st down from these swelling Heavens,
220		I am too perfect in: and but for shame,
		In such a parley should I answere thee.

THE LADY AGAINE IN WELSH

	Mortimer	I understand thy Kisses, and thou mine,	
		And that's a feeling disputation:	
		But I will never be a Truant, Love,	
225		Till I have learn'd thy Language: for thy tongue	R 61 - a (or j)
		Makes Welsh as sweet as Ditties highly penn'd,	
		Sung by a faire Queene in a Summers Bowre,	
		With ravishing Division to her Lute.	

	Glendower	Nay, if *thou melt, then will she runne madde.

THE LADY SPEAKES AGAINE IN WELSH

230	Mortimer	O, I am Ignorance it selfe in this.

	Glendower	She bids you, → [2]
		On the wanton Rushes lay you downe,
		And rest your gentle Head upon her Lappe,
		And she will sing the Song that pleaseth you,
235		And on your Eye-lids Crowne the God of Sleepe,
		Charming your blood with pleasing heavinesse;
		Making such difference betwixt [3] Wake and Sleepe,
		As is the difference betwixt Day and Night,
		The houre before the Heavenly Harneis'd Teeme
240		Begins his Golden Progresse in the East.

[VP] [1]
most modern texts partially follow Qq here and set the whole speech in prose, though Qq do seem to set the first line in verse, and then the rest in one long prose line

[SP] [2]
most modern texts follow Qq and turn these two short Ff lines into one split verse line, though this Ff setting allows for Glendower to react before passing his daughter's thoughts on to Mortimer

[W] [3]
Q1 - 3 and most modern texts = 'twixt', Q4 - 5/Ff = 'betwixt'

	Mortimer	With all my heart Ile sit, and heare her sing:
		By that time will our Booke, I thinke, be drawne.
	Glendower	Doe so : →¹
		And those Musitians that shall play to you,
245		Hang in the Ayre a thousand Leagues from thence; ²
		And straight they shall be here: sit, and attend.
	Hotspurre	Come Kate, thou art perfect in lying downe:
		Come, quicke, quicke, that I may lay my Head in thy
		Lappe. ³
250	**Lady**	Goe, ye giddy-Goose.

THE MUSICKE PLAYES

	Hotspurre	Now I perceive the Devill understands Welsh,
		And 'tis no marvell he is so humorous:
		Byrlady *hee's a good Musitian.
	Lady	Then would you be nothing but Musicall,
255		For you are altogether governed by humors:
		Lye still ye Theefe, and heare the Lady sing in Welsh. ⁴
	Hotspurre	I had rather heare (Lady) my Brach howle in
		Irish.
	Lady	Would'st⁵ have thy Head broken?
260	**Hotspurre**	No.
	Lady	Then be still.
	Hotspurre	Neyther, 'tis a Womans fault.
	Lady	Now God helpe thee.
	Hotspurre	To the Welsh Ladies Bed.
265	**Lady**	What's that?

SP ¹ most modern texts follow Qq and set Ff's two short lines as one line of split verse, though the Ff setting may allow Glendower a moment of 'magic' or ritual before, after, or even as he begins to speak

W ² Q1 - 3 = 'hence', Q4 - 5/Ff = 'thence'

VP ³ though Qq/Ff set the passage in verse as shown, some modern texts set it as prose: this is a shame, for it then wipes out the definite prose passage between them a little later, lines 282-5, where (presumably) the intimacy of prose rather than the formality of the verse is really required

VP ⁴ ditto

W ⁵ most modern texts follow Q1 - 2 and set 'thou', omitted by Q3 - 5/Ff

Hotspurre	Peace, shee sings.

HEERE THE LADY SINGS A WELSH SONG

Hotspurre	Come, Ile have your Song too.
Lady	Not mine, in good sooth.
Hotspurre	Not yours, in good sooth? ᵗ ¹

270   You sweare like a Comfit-makers Wife:
Not you, in good sooth; and, as true as I live;
And, as God shall mend me; and, as sure as day: ²
And givest such Sarcenet suretie for thy Oathes,
As if thou never walk'st further then Finsbury.

275   Sweare me, Kate, like a Lady, as thou art,
A good mouth-filling Oath: and leave in sooth,
And such protest of Pepper Ginger-bread,
To Velvet-Guards, and Sunday-Citizens.

Come, sing.

280 **Lady**	I will not sing.

Hotspurre	'Tis the next way to turne Taylor, or be Red-

brest teacher: and the Indentures be drawne, Ile away   L 62 - a (or j)
within these two howres: and so come in, when yee
will.

285 **Glendower**   Come, come, Lord Mortimer, you are as slow,
As hot Lord Percy is on fire to goe.

By this our Booke is drawne: wee'le but seale,
And then to Horse immediately.

Mortimer	With all my heart.

[Exeunt]

ᵂ ₁ most modern texts follow Qq and set 'Hart' (i.e. 'Heart'), omitted by Ff

ᵛᴾ ₂ most modern texts follow Qq and set the speech to this point in prose, with the rest continuing in verse: this seems somewhat of a shame, for Hotspurre's next reaction to her refusal to sing is set in prose in Ff: thus Ff offer a nice delineation between the underlying manner of his different reactions, especially after being refused a second time

Scœna Secunda

ENTER THE KING, PRINCE OF WALES, AND OTHERS

King		Lords, give us leave:

> The Prince of Wales, and I,°
> Must have some private conference:
> But be neere at hand,° ¹

5   For wee shall presently have neede of you.

[Exeunt Lords]

                   I know not whether 'Heaven will have it so,
                   For some displeasing service I have done;
                   That in this secret Doome, out of my Blood,
                   Hee'le breede Revengement, and a Scourge for me:
10   But thou do'st in thy passages of Life,
                   Make me beleeve, that thou art onely mark'd
                   For the hot vengeance, and the Rod of heaven
                   To punish my Mistreadings.   Tell me else,
15   Could such inordinate and low desires,
                   Such poore, such bare, such lewd, such meane attempts,
                   Such barren pleasures, rude societie,
                   As thou art matcht withall, and grafted too,²
                   Accompanie the greatnesse of thy blood,
20   And hold their levell with thy Princely heart?

Prince   So please your Majesty, I would I could
                   Quit all offences with as cleare excuse,
                   As well as I am doubtlesse I can purge
                   My selfe of many I am charg'd withall:
25   Yet such extenuation let me begge,
                   As in reproofe of many Tales devis'd,
                   Which oft the Eare of Greatnesse needes must heare,
                   By smiling Pick-thankes, and base Newes-mongers;

---

^LS ₁ most modern texts follow Qq and set the opening scene as the symbol ° shows: the rather peculiar second of the 10/13/10 syllable structure suggests the King momentarily loses his self-control: the gaps of the Ff setting (4/6/8/5/10) suggest he is doing the exact opposite, viz. being very careful to maintain his self-control

^W ₂ most modern texts follow Qq and set 'grafted to', Ff = 'grafted too'

30		I may for some things true, wherein my youth Hath faultie wandred, and irregular, Finde pardon on my true submission.

          King   'Heaven pardon thee: → [1]
                            Yet let me wonder, Harry,
                            At thy affections, which doe hold a Wing

35   Quite from the flight of all thy ancestors.

                            Thy place in Councell thou hast rudely lost,
                            Which by thy younger Brother is supply'de;
                            And art almost an alien to the hearts
                            Of all the Court and Princes of my blood.

40   The hope and expectation of thy time
                            Is ruin'd, and the Soule of every man
                            Prophetically doe fore-thinke thy fall.

                            Had I so lavish of my presence beene,
                            So common hackney'd in the eyes of men,

45   So stale and cheape to vulgar Company;
                            Opinion, that did helpe me to the Crowne,
                            Had still kept loyall to possession,
                            And left me in reputelesse banishment,
                            A fellow of no marke, nor likelyhood.

50   By being seldome seeme, I could not stirre,
                            But like a Comet, I was wondred at,   R 62 - a (or j)
                            The men would tell their Children, This is hee:
                            Others would say; Where, Which is Bullingbrooke.

                            And then I stole all Courtesie from Heaven,

55   And drest my selfe in such Humilitie,
                            That I did plucke Allegeance from mens hearts,
                            Lowd Showts and Salutations from their mouthes,
                            Even in the presence of the Crowned King.

                            Thus I did [2] keepe my Person fresh and new,

60   My Presence like a Robe Pontificall,
                            Ne're seene, but wondred at: and so my State,
                            Seldome but sumptuous, shewed like a Feast,
                            And wonne [3] by rarenesse such Solemnitie.

R 62 - a (or j) / L 63 - a (or j) : 3. 2. 26 - 59

[SP 1] as the opening to the scene, most modern texts follow Qq and set as a single line what Ff show as two short lines: the Ff setting again seems to suggest the King is taking a pause in an attempt to control himself, something not evident in the single line setting

[2] Q1 - 4 and most modern texts = 'did I', Q5/Ff = 'I did'

[3] some modern texts follow Qq and set a past tense form of the verb 'to win', viz. 'wan', Ff = 'wonne'

The skipping King hee ambled up and downe,
65   With shallow Jesters, and rash Bavin Wits,
Soone kindled, and soone burnt, carded his State,
Mingled his Royaltie with Carping [1] Fooles,
Had his great Name prophaned with their Scornes,
And gave his Countenance, against his Name,
70   To laugh at gybing Boyes, and stand the push
Of every Beardlesse vaine Comparative;
Grew a Companion to the common Streetes,
Enfeoff'd himselfe to Popularitie:
That being dayly swallowed by mens Eyes,
75   They surfeted with Honey, and began to loathe [2]
The taste of Sweetnesse, whereof a little
More then a little, is by much too much.

So when he had occasion to be seene,
He was but as a Cuckow is in June,
80   Heard, not regarded: seene but with such Eyes,
As sicke and blunted with Communitie,
Affoord no extraordinarie Gaze,
Such as is bent on Sunne-like Majestie,
When it shines seldome in admiring Eyes:
85   But rather drowz'd, and hung their eye-lids downe,
Slept in his Face, and rendred such aspect
As Cloudie men use to doe [3] to their adversaries,
Being with his presence glutted, gorg'd, and full.

And in that very Line, Harry, standest thou:
90   For thou hast lost thy Princely Priviledge,
With vile participation.
                  Not an Eye
But is awearie of thy common sight,
Save mine, which hath desir'd to see thee more:
95   Which now doth that I would not have it doe,
Make blinde it selfe with foolish tendernesse.

Prince   I shall hereafter, my thrice gracious Lord,
Be more my selfe.
                }

W [1] Q1 = 'capring' (i.e. capering), Ff = 'Carping'

LS [2] though Qq/Ff set the 12 syllable line as shown, most modern texts take the last two words 'to loathe' and place them at the beginning of the following line, thus maintaining the pentameter of this line while turning the following line into 12 syllables: by keeping the original structure the loss of control comes on the much stronger image as written, viz. 'loathe' rather than anything in the following line

W [3] most modern texts follow Q1 - 2 and omit 'to do' as set in Q3 - 5/F1: F2 - 4 = 'use to do their'

	King	For all the World,
100		As thou art to this houre, was Richard then,
		When I from France set foot at Ravenspurgh ;
		And even as I was then, is Percy now :
		Now by my Scepter, and my Soule to boot,
		He hath more worthy interest to the State
105		Then thou, the shadow of Succession ;
		For of no Right, nor colour like to Right.

He doth fill fields with Harneis in the Realme,
Turnes head against the Lyons armed Jawes ;
And being no more in debt to yeeres, then thou,
110 Leades ancient Lords, and reverent Bishops on
To bloody Battailes, and to brusing Armes.

What never-dying Honor hath he got,
Against renowned Dowglas? whose high Deedes,
Whose hot Incursions, and great Name in Armes,
115 Holds from all Souldiers chiefe Majoritie,
And Militarie Title Capitall.

Through all the Kingdomes that acknowledge Christ,[1]
Thrice hath the [2] Hotspur Mars, in swathing [3] Clothes,   L 63 - a (or j)
This Infant Warrior, in his Enterprises,
120 Discomfited great Dowglas, ta'ne him once,
Enlarged him, and made a friend of him,
To fill the mouth of deepe Defiance up,
And shake the peace and safetie of our Throne.

And what say you to this?
125   Percy, Northumberland,
The Arch-bishops Grace of Yorke, Dowglas, Mortimer,
Capitulate against us, and are up.

But wherefore doe I tell these Newes to thee?

Why, Harry, doe I tell thee of my Foes,
130 Which art my *neer'st and dearest Enemie?

Thou, that art like enough, through vassall Feare,
Base Inclination, and the start of Spleene,
To fight against me under Percies pay,
To dogge his heeles, and curtsie at his frownes,
135 To shew how much thou art degenerate. [4]

L 63 - a (or j) / R 63 - a (or j) : 3. 2. 93 - 128

PCT [1] most modern texts follow Q1 - 3 and end the sentence here, starting a fresh sentence with 'Thrice hath this . . .'

W [2] Q1 - 4 = 'this', Q5/Ff = 'the'

W [3] Q1 - 3 and most modern texts = 'swathling' (i.e. 'swaddling'), Q4 - 5/Ff = 'swathing'

IST [4] this passage could be set as anywhere between two and five sentences long

Prince		Doe†¹ not thihke so, you shall not finde it so:
		And ˙Heaven forgive them, that so much have sway'd
		Your Majesties good thoughts away from me:
		I will redeeme all this on Percies head,
140		And in the closing of some glorious day,
		Be bold to tell you, that I am your Sonne,
		When I will weare a Garment all of Blood,
		And staine my favours in a bloody Maske:
		Which washt away, shall scowre my shame with it.

And that shall be the day, when ere it lights,
That this same Child of Honor and Renowne,
This gallant Hotspur, this all-praysed Knight,
And your unthought-of Harry chance to meet:
For every Honor fitting² on his Helme,
Would they were multitudes, and on my head
My shame redoubled.   For the time will come,
That I shall make this Northerne Youth exchange
His glorious Deedes for my Indignities:
Percy is but my Factor, good my Lord,
To engrosse up glorious Deedes on my behalfe:
And I will call him to so strict account,
That he shall render every Glory up,
Yea, even the sleightest worship of his time,
Or I will teare the Reckoning from his Heart.

This, in the Name of ˙Heaven, I promise here:
The which, if I performe, and doe survive,³
I doe beseech your Majestie, may salve
The long-growne Wounds of my intemperature: ⁴
If not, the end of Life cancells all Bands,
And I will dye a hundred thousand Deaths,
Ere breake the smallest parcell of this Vow.

King A hundred thousand Rebels dye in this:
Thou shalt have Charge, and soveraigne trust herein.

ENTER BLUNT

How now good Blunt? thy Lookes are full of speed.

ᵂ₁ F1 = 'D oe', F2/most modern texts = 'Doe'

ᵂ₂ Q1 - 3/F2 and most modern texts = 'sitting', F1 = 'fitting'

ᴼ/ᵂ₃ Qq and most modern texts = 'This in the name of God I promise heere/The which if he be pleasd I shall performe:' F1 = 'This, in the name of Heaven, I promise here:/The which, if I performe and doe survive', F2 -4 start the second line with 'The which, if I promise'

ᵂ₄ Qq = 'intemperance', Ff = 'intemperature'

Blunt	So hath the Businesse that I come to speake of.
	Lord Mortimer of Scotland hath sent word,
	That Dowglas and the English Rebels met
	The eleventh of this moneth, at Shrewsbury:
175	A mightie and a fearefull Head they are,
	(If Promises be kept on every hand)
	As ever offered foule play in a State.
King	The Earle of Westmerland set forth to day:
	With him my sonne, Lord John of Lancaster,
180	For this advertisement is five dayes old.
	On Wednesday next, Harry thou shalt [1] set forward:
	On Thursday, wee our selves will march. [2]

Our meeting is Bridgenorth: and Harry, you shall march   R 63 - a (or j)
Through Glocestershire: by which account,
185   Our Businesse valued some twelve dayes hence,
Our generall Forces at Bridgenorth shall meete.

Our Hands are full of Businesse: let's away,
Advantage feedes him fat, while men delay.

[Exeunt]

[W] [1] Q1 - 2 and most modern texts = 'you shall', Q3 - 5/Ff = 'thou shalt'

[LS] [2] Qq = 'On thursday we our selves will march. Our meeting/ls': some modern texts agree with Ff but restructure the next line to 'Our meeting is Bridgenorth, and Harry, you/Shall march': Ff's pause plus long line have wonderful theatrical/character impact as the King's plans are at last successfully completed

Scena Tertia

ENTER FALSTAFFE AND BARDOLPH [1]

Falstaffe	Bardolph, am I not falne away vilely, since this
	last action? doe I not bate? doe I not dwindle?
	Why
	my skinne hangs about me like an olde Ladies loose
5	Gowne : I am withered like an old AppleJohn.
	Well,
	Ile repent, and that suddenly, while I am in some liking :
	I shall be out of heart shortly, and then I shall have no
	strength to repent.
10	And I have not forgotten what the
	in-side of a Church is made of, I am a Pepper-Corne, a
	Brewers Horse, the in-side of a Church.
	Company, villa-
	nous Company hath beene the spoyle ofme.
15 **Bardolph**	Sir John, you are so fretfull, you cannot live
	long.
Falstaffe	Why there it is : Come, sing me a bawdy Song,
	make me merry : I was as vertuously given, as a Gentle-
	man need to be ; vertuous enough, swore little, dic'd not
20	above seven times [2] a weeke, went to a Bawdy-house not
	above once [3] in a quarter of an houre, payd Money that I
	borrowed,[4] three or four times ; lived well, and in good
	compasse : and now I live out of all order, out of com-
	passe.
25 **Bardolph**	Why, you are so fat, Sir John, that you must
	needes bee out of all compasse ; out of all reasonable
	compasse Sir John.

[SD][1] because of a later stage direction, some modern texts add that Falstaffe is carrying a Truncheon, a sign of his new Office

[PCT][2] most modern texts add a dash here to illustrate the timing as Falstaffe qualifies the first part of his statement, turning the apparent seriousness of it into a joke

[PCT][3] ditto

[PCT][4] ditto

Falstaffe	Doe thou amend thy Face, and Ile amend thy [1]
	Life : Thou art our Admirall, thou bearest the Lanterne
30		in the Poope, but 'tis in the Nose of thee ; thou art the
	Knight of the burning Lampe.
Bardolph	Why, Sir John, my Face does you no harme.
Falstaffe	No, Ile be sworne : I make as good use of it, as
	many a man doth of a Deaths-Head, or a *Memento Mori*.
35		I never see thy Face, but I thinke upon Hell fire, and Dives
	that lived in Purple ; for there he is in his Robes burning,
	burning.
	If thou wert any way given to vertue, I would
	sweare by thy Face ; my Oath should bee, *By this Fire* : [2]
40		But thou art altogether given over ; and wert indeede,
	but for the Light in thy Face, the Sunne [3] of utter Darke-
	nesse.
	When thou ran'st up Gads-Hill in the Night, to
	catch my Horse, if I did not thinke that [4] thou hadst beene
45		an *Ignis fatuus*, or a Ball of Wild-fire, there's no Purchase
	in Money.
	O, thou art a perpetuall Triumph, an ever-
	lasting Bone-fire-Light : thou hast saved me a thousand
	Markes in Linkes and Torches, walking with thee in the
50		Night betwixt Taverne and Taverne : But the Sack that
	thou hast drunke me, would have bought me Lights as
	good cheape, as [5] the dearest Chandlers in Europe.
	I have
	maintain'd that Salamander of yours with fire, any time
55		this two and thirtie yeeres, *Heaven reward me for it.
Bardolph	[6] I would my Face were in your Belly.
Falstaffe	[7] So should I be sure to be heart-burn'd.

ENTER HOSTESSE

How now, Dame Parltet the Hen, have you enquir'd yet
who pick'd my Pocket?   L 64 - a (or j)

L 64 - a (or j) : 3. 3. 24 - 53

[w][1] Ff = 'thy', Qq/most modern texts = 'my'

[o][2] most modern texts follow Q3 - 5 and set the oath omitted by Ff, 'thats Gods Angell'

[w][3] most modern texts follow Qq and set 'sonne', thus preserving the pun; Ff = 'Sunne'

[w][4] most modern texts follow Q1 - 2 and omit 'that', which Q3 - 5/Ff set

[w][5] Q1 - 4 and most modern texts = 'at', Q5/Ff = 'as'

[o][6] most modern texts follow Qq and set the oath omitted by Ff, 'Zbloud,'

[o][7] most modern texts follow Qq and set the oath omitted by Ff, 'Godamercy,'

60	**Hostesse**	Why Sir John, what doe you thinke, Sir John?
		doe you thinke I keepe Theeves in my House?
		I have
		search'd, I have enquired, so haz my Husband, Man by
		Man, Boy by Boy, Servant by Servant: the tight [1] of a
65		hayre was never lost in my house before.
	Falstaffe	Ye lye Hostesse: Bardolph was shav'd, and lost
		many a hayre; and Ile be sworne my Pocket was pick'd:
		goe to, you are a Woman, goe.
	Hostesse	Who I?
70		[2] I defie thee: [3] I was never call'd so
		in mine owne house before.
	Falstaffe	Goe to, I know you well enough.
	Hostesse	No, Sir John, you doe not know me, Sir John:
		I know you, Sir John: you owe me Money, Sir John, and
75		now you picke a quarrell, to beguile me of it: I bought
		you a dozen Shirts to your Backe.
	Falstaffe	Doulas, filthy Doulas: I have given them
		away to Bakers Wives, and [4] they have made Boulters of
		them.
80	**Hostesse**	Now as I am a true Woman, Holland of eight
		shillings an Ell: You owe Money here besides, Sir John,
		for your Dyet, and by-Drinkings, and Money lent you,
		foure and twentie pounds. [5]
	Falstaffe	Hee had his part of it, let him pay.
85	**Hostesse**	Hee? alas hee is poore, hee hath no-
		thing.
	Falstaffe	How?
		Poore?
		Looke upon his Face: What call
90		you Rich?
		Let them coyne his Nose, let them coyne his
		Cheekes, Ile not pay a Denier.

W [1] most modern texts = 'tithe', Qq/Ff = 'tight'

W [2] most modern texts follow Q1 - 4 and set 'No', which Q5/Ff omit

O [3] most modern texts follow Qq and set the oath omitted by Ff, 'Gods light'

W [4] most modern texts follow Qq and omit 'and' as set by Ff

W [5] Qq and most modern texts = 'pound', Ff = 'pounds'

What, will you make a
Younker of me?
95   Shall I not take mine ease in mine Inne,
but I shall have my Pocket pick'd?
                 I have lost a Seale-
Ring of my Grand-fathers, worth fortie Marke.

Hostesse	[1] I have heard the Prince tell him, I know not
100		how oft, that the Ring was Copper.
Falstaffe	How? the Prince is a Jacke, a Sneake-Cuppe: [2]
	and if [3] hee were heere, I would cudgell him like a Dogge,
	if hee would say so.

**ENTER THE PRINCE MARCHING, [4] AND FALSTAFFE MEETS
HIM, PLAYING ON HIS TRUNCHION
LIKE A FIFE**

Falstaffe	How now Lad? is the Winde in that Doore? [5]
105		Must we all march?
Bardolph	Yea, two and two, Newgate fashion.
Hostesse	My Lord, I pray you heare me.

> **Prince**   What say'st thou, Mistresse Quickly?
>   How
> 110   does [6] thy Husband? °
>   I love him well, hee is an honest
> man. ° [7]

Hostesse	Good, my Lord, heare mee.
Falstaffe	Prethee let her alone, and list to mee.
115	**Prince**	What say'st thou, Jacke?
Falstaffe	The other Night I fell asleepe heere behind the
	Arras, and had my Pocket pickt: this House is turn'd
	Bawdy-house, they picke Pockets.

° 1 most modern texts follow Qq and set the oath omitted by Ff, 'O Jesu,'

W 2 most modern texts follow Q1 - 2 and set 'sneakeup', Q3 - 5/Ff = 'Sneake-Cuppe'

° 3 Qq and most modern texts = 'Zblood and', Ff = 'and if'

SD 4 since the Prince talks to him in his last speech in the scene, most modern texts add Peto to the entry (or Harvey instead)

° 5 most modern texts follow Qq and set the oath omitted by Ff, 'ifaith'

W 6 Q1/Q4 = 'doth', Q2-3 = 'doeth', Ff = 'does'

VP 7 though Qq/Ff set prose, at least one text suggests the Prince greets the Hostesse in verse

Prince	What didst thou lose, Jacke?	
120 **Falstaffe**	Wilt thou beleeve me, Hal?	
	Three or foure Bonds	
	of fortie pound apeece, and a Seale-Ring of my Grand-	
	fathers.	
Prince	A Trifle, some eight-penny matter.	
125 **Hostesse**	So I told him, my Lord ; and I said, I heard your	
	Grace say so : and (my Lord) hee speakes most vilely of	
	you, like a foule-mouth'd man as hee is, and said, hee	
	would cudgell you.	
Prince	What hee did not?	
130 **Hostesse**	There's neyther Faith, Truth, nor Woman-hood	
	in me else.	R 64 - a (or j)
Falstaffe	There's no more faith in thee then [1] a stu'de Prune ;	
	nore no more truth in thee, then in a drawne Fox : and for	
	Wooman-hood, Maid-marian may be the Deputies wife	
135	of the Ward to thee.	
	Go you nothing : [2] go.	
Falstaffe	Say, what thing? what thing?	
Falstaffe	What thing? why a thing to thanke *heaven on.	
Hostesse	I am no thing to thanke *heaven on, I wold thou	
140	shouldst know it : I am an honest mans wife : and setting	
	thy Knighthood aside, thou art a knave to call me so.	
Falstaffe	Setting thy woman-hood aside, thou art a beast	
	to say otherwise.	
Hostesse	Say, what beast, thou knave thou?	
145 **Falstaffe**	What beast?	
	Why an Otter.	
Prince	An Otter, sir John?	
	Why an Otter?	
Falstaffe	Why?	
150	She's neither fish nor flesh ; a man knowes	
	not where to have her.	

R 64 - a (or j) / L 65 - a (or j) :   3. 3. 100 - 128

[1] some modern texts follow Q1/F3 and add 'in', omitted by Q2 - 5/F1 - 2

[2] Qq and most modern texts = 'thing', Ff = 'nothing'

	Hostesse	Thou art [1] unjust man in saying so; thou, or anie man knowes where to have me, thou knave thou.
155	Prince	Thou say'st true Hostesse, and he slanders thee most grossely.
	Hostesse	So he doth you, my Lord, and sayde this other day, You ought him a thousand pound.
	Prince	Sirrah, do I owe you a thousand pound?
160	Falstaffe	A thousand pound Hal? A Million. Thy love is worth a Million: thou ow'st me thy love.
	Hostesse	Nay my Lord, he call'd you Jacke, and said hee would cudgell you.
165	Falstaffe	Did I, Bardolph?
	Bardolph	Indeed Sir John, you said so.
	Falstaffe	Yea, if he said my ring was Copper.
170	Prince	I say 'tis Copper. Dar'st thou bee as good as my word now?
	Falstaffe	Why Hal? thou know'st, as thou art but a [2] man, I dare: but, as thou art a [3] Prince, I feare thee, as I feare the roaring of the Lyons Whelpe.
	Prince	And why not as the Lyon?
175	Falstaffe	The King himselfe is to bee feared as the Lyon: Do'st thou thinke Ile feare thee, as I feare thy Father? nay if [4] I do, [5] let my Girdle breake.

[1] most modern texts follow Qq/F3 and add 'an', omitted by F1 - 2

[2] most modern texts follow Qq and omit 'a', set by Ff

[3] ditto

[4] Qq and most modern texts = 'and', Ff = 'if'

[5] most modern texts follow Qq and set the oath, 'I pray God', Ff = 'let'

Prince	O, if it should. [1] how would thy guttes fall about
	thy knees.
180	But sirra: There's no roome for Faith, Truth,
	nor Honesty, in this bosome of thine: it is all fill'd uppe
	with Guttes and Midriffe.
	Charge an honest Woman
	with picking thy pocket?
185	Why thou horson impudent
	imbost Rascall, if there were any thing in thy Pocket but
	Taverne Recknings, Memorandums of Bawdie-houses,
	and one poore peny-worth of Sugar-candie to make thee
	long-winded: if thy pocket were enrich'd with anie o-
190	ther injuries but these, I am a Villaine: And yet you will
	stand to it, you will not Pocket up wrong.
	Art thou not
	asham'd?
Falstaffe	Do'st thou heare Hal?
195	Thou know'st in the state
	of Innocency, Adam fell: and what should poore Jacke
	Falstaffe do, in the dayes of Villany?
	Thou seest, I have
	more flesh then another man, and therefore more frailty.
200	You confesse then you pickt my Pocket?
Prince	It appeares so by the Story.
Falstaffe	[2] Hostesse, I forgive thee:
	Go make ready Breakfast, love thy Husband,
	Looke to thy Servants, and [3] cherish thy Guests:
205	Thou shalt find me tractable to any honest reason:
	Thou seest, I am pacified still.
	Nay, I [4] prethee be gone.

[Exit Hostesse]

Now Hal, to the newes at Court [5] for the Robbery, Lad?

How is that answered?   L 65 - a (or j)

}

PCT[1] Qq/F2 and all modern texts set a comma, F1 sets a (most peculiar) period

VP[2] Ff set this speech plus the Prince's reply in exuberant verse: Qq and most modern texts set prose

▼[3] modern texts follow Qq and omit 'and' as set by Ff

▼[4] most modern texts follow Q1 - 4 and omit 'I' as set by Q5/Ff

PCT[5] though Qq/Ff set no punctuation, some modern texts set a period or a colon here

210	**Prince**	O my sweet Beefe : I must still be good Angell to thee. The Monie is paid backe againe.
	Falstaffe	O, I do not like that paying backe, 'tis a double Labour.
215	**Prince**	I am good Friends with my Father, and may do any thing.
	Falstaffe	Rob me the Exchequer the first thing thou do'st, and do it with unwash'd hands too.
	Bardolph	Do my Lord.
220	**Prince**	I have procured thee Jacke, a Charge of Foot.

	Falstaffe	I would it had been of Horse.
		                          Where shal I finde
		 one that can steale well?
		                    O, for a fine theefe of ¹ two and

225		twentie, or •thereabout : I am heynously unprovided.
		                                      Wel
		 God be thanked for these Rebels, they offend none but
		 the Vertuous.
		           I laud them, I praise them.

230	**Prince**	Bardolph.
	Bardolph	My Lord.
	Prince	Go beare this Letter to Lord John of Lancaster To my Brother John. This to my Lord of Westmerland,²
235		³ Go Peto, to horse : ⁴ for thou, and I, Have thirtie miles to ride yet ere dinner time.
240		Jacke, meet me to morrow in the Temple Hall At two •a clocke in the afternoone, There shalt thou know thy Charge, and there receive Money and Order for their Furniture.

ᵂ ₁ Qq and most modern texts set 'the age of', omitted by Ff

ˢᴰ ₂ most modern texts add a stage direction here for Bardolph's exit, and another for Peto at the end of the next sentence

ⱽᴾ/ᴾ ₃ though Qq/Ff set this speech as verse, some modern texts remove its excitement by reducing it to prose: also, at least one text replaces 'Peto' with 'Harvey'

ᵂ ₄ most modern texts follow Q1 - 2 and add an extra 'to horse', omitted in Q3 - 5/Ff

The Land is burning, Percie stands on hye,
And either they, or we [1] must lower lye. [†2]

Falstaffe   Rare words! brave world. → [3]

245
Hostesse, my breakfast, come:
Oh, I could wish this Taverne were my drumme.

[Exeunt omnes]

R 65 - a (or j)   :   3. 3. 203 - 206

[W1] Q1 - 3 = 'we or they', Q4 - 5/Ff = 'they, or we'

[W2] F1 = 'l ye', F2/most modern texts = 'lye'

[SP3] most modern texts follow Qq and set Ff's two short lines as one verse line: Ff's pause gives Falstaffe time for his final bravado, before turning his attention to more mundane matters

Actus Quartus. Scœna Prima

ENTER HARRIE HOTSPURRE, WORCESTER,
AND DOWGLAS

Hotspurre	Well said, my Noble Scot, if speaking truth
	In this fine Age, were not thought flatterie,
	Such attribution should the Dowglas have,
	As not a Souldiour of this seasons stampe,
	Should go so generall currant through the world.

By °heaven I cannot flatter: I¹ defie
The Tongues of Soothers.
                                          But a Braver place
In my hearts love, hath no man then your Selfe.

Nay, taske me to my word: approve me Lord.

Dowglas	Thou art the King of Honor:
	No man so potent breathes upon the ground,
	But I will Beard him.

ENTER A MESSENGER

Hotspurre	Do so, and 'tis well. °
	What Letters hast² there?
	I can but thanke you. °
Messenger	These Letters come from your Father.
Hotspurre	Letters from him?
	Why comes he not himselfe? °
Messenger	He cannot come, my Lord,
	He is greevous sicke. ° ³

Line numbers: 5, 10, 15, 20

ᵂ₁ most modern texts follow Q1 and set 'do', omitted by Q2 - 5/Ff

ᵂ₂ Qq/some modern texts set 'thou', Ff omit the word

ᴸˢ₃ the Ff/Qq texts allow a gap (5/10 syllables) for the entrance of the Messenger, which most modern texts
eradicate: Ff then allow a gap both before and after the Messenger first speaks (6/8 syllables), which is not shown
in either Qq or the modern texts: Ff then allow for quick debate between Hotspurre and the Messenger via the
split lines - which are also not set in Qq or the modern texts

Hotspurre	¹ How? haz he the leysure to be sicke now,²	
	In such a justling time?	
	Who leades his power?	
25	Under whose Government†³ come they along ?	R 65 - a (or j)
Messenger	His Letters beares ⁴ his minde, not I his minde. ⁵	
Worcester	I prethee tell me, doth he keepe his Bed?	
Messenger	He did, my Lord, foure dayes ere I set forth :	
	And at the time of my departure thence,	
30	He was much fear'd by his Physician. ⁶	
Worcester	I would the state of time had first beene whole,	
	Ere he by sicknesse had beene visited :	
	His health was never better worth then now.	
Hotspurre	Sicke now? droope now? this sicknes doth infect	
35	The very Life-blood of our Enterprise,	
	'Tis catching hither, even to our Campe.	

> ⁷ He writes me here, that inward sicknesse,
> And that his friends by deputation
> Could not° so soone be drawne :   nor did he thinke it meet,°

40	To lay so dangerous and deare a trust
	On any Soule remov'd, but on his owne.
	Yet doth he give us bold advertisement,
	That with our small conjunction we should on,
	To see how Fortune is dispos'd to us :
45	For, as he writes, there is no quailing now,
	Because the King is certainely possest
	Of all our purposes.
	What say you to it?

° ₁ most modern texts follow Qq and set the oath omitted by Ff, 'Zounds,'

W ₂ most modern texts follow Qq and omit 'now' as set by Ff, presumably arguing that since Ff had not set the oath 'Zounds' (footnote #1 above) an extra word had to be added to maintain the pentameter

W ₃ Qq/F2 /all modern texts = 'government', F1 = 'Gonerment' (i.e. the 'u' used as 'v' was set upside down)

W ₄ Qq/Ff = 'beares', most modern texts = 'bear'

W ₅ Q1 - 2 = 'not I my mind', Q3 - 5/Ff = 'not I his mind', most modern texts = 'not I, my Lord'

W ₆ Q1 - 3 and most modern texts = 'Physitions', Q4 - 5/Ff = 'Physician'

W/LS/ADD ₇ since the next passage does not follow on with complete logic, many scholars suggest some lines have been lost from here (at the very least commentators suggest adding the direction 'stays him' or 'holds him' to the start of this line): this is not necessarily so, for Hotspurre's incoherence in times of stress has already been seen throughout the play, and this is probably another fine example of it: this possibility is heightened when the next two irregular Qq/Ff lines (9 -10/12 syllables) are taken into account: however, most modern texts readjust the lines as shown (11 or 12/11 syllables) thus somewhat regularising a further moment of loss of control

	Worcester	Your Fathers sicknesse is a mayme to us.
50	**Hotspurre**	A perillous Gash, a very Limme lopt off:
		And yet, in faith, it is not his present want

Seemes more then we shall finde it.

Were it good,° to set the exact wealth of all our states° 1

All at one Cast?

55   To set so rich a mayne

On the nice hazard of one doubtfull houre,²

It were not good: for therein should we reade

The very Bottome, and the Soule of Hope,

The very List, the very utmost Bound

60   Of all our fortunes.

	Dowglas	Faith, and so wee should,
		Where now remaines° a sweet reversion.

We may boldly spend,° upon the hope

Of what is to come in: ° 3

65   A comfort of retyrement lives in this.

	Hotspurre	A Randevous, a Home to flye unto,
		If that the Devill and Mischance looke bigge
		Upon the Maydenhead of our Affaires.
	Worcester	But yet I would your Father had beene here:
70		The Qualitie and Heire ⁴ of our Attempt
		Brookes no division: It will be thought
		By some, that know not why he is away,
		That wisedome, loyaltie, and meere dislike
		Of our proceedings, kept the Earle from hence.
75		And thinke, how such an apprehension
		May turne the tyde of fearefull Faction,
		And breede a kinde of question in our cause:
		For well you know, wee of the offring side,
		Must keepe aloofe from strict arbitrement,

L 66 - a (or j) : 4. 1. 42 - 70

LS 1   Ff again set another 'loss of control' moment for Hotspurre, (7/13 syllables): most modern texts follow Qq and adjust the passage to two regular pentameter lines as shown

PCT 2   most modern texts follow Q1 - 2 and set a question mark here, thus starting the next line with a new 'answering' sentence: Q3 - 5/Ff set a comma, allowing the sentence to continue

LS 3   as Dowglas attempts to convey his own enthusiasm despite the poor odds, both Qq and Ff set an awkward series of moments (perhaps there is a lack of expected reaction from the others, perhaps he is persuading himself): Ff's setting (5 syllables as the second part of a split line/9 or 10/9/6), allows an enthusiastic shared split line start and a hesitation towards the end: most modern texts follow Qq and set the passage as 5/8/10 or 11/10 syllables, thus creating a more hesitant start and a more confident finish

W 4   Q1 - 3 and most modern texts = 'haire', Q4 = 'heaire', Q5/Ff = 'Heire'

80		And stop all sight-holes, every loope, from whence
		The eye of reason may prie in upon us:
		This absence of your Father [1] drawes a Curtaine,
		That shewes the ignorant a kinde of feare,
		Before not dreamt of.
85	**Hotspurre**	You strayne too farre.
		I rather of his absence make this use:
		It lends a Lustre, and more great Opinion,
		A larger Date to your [2] great Enterprize,
		Then if the Earle were here: for men must thinke,
90		If we without his helpe, can make a Head
		To push against the [3] Kingdome; with his helpe,
		We shall o're-turne [4] it topsie-turvy downe:
		Yet all goes well, yet all our joynts are whole.

L 66 - a (or j)

	Dowglas	As heart can thinke:
95		There is not such a word° spoke of in Scotland,
		At [5] this Dreame [6] of Feare. ° [7]

ENTER SIR RICHARD VERNON

	Hotspurre	My Cousin Vernon, welcome by my Soule.
	Vernon	Pray God my newes be worth a welcome, Lord,
		The Earle of Westmerland, seven thousand strong,
100		Is marching hither-wards, with [8] Prince John.
	Hotspurre	No harme: what more?
	Vernon	And further, I have learn'd,
		The King himselfe in person hath [9] set forth,
		Or hither-wards intended speedily,
105		With strong and mightie preparation.

L 66 - a (or j) / R 66 - a (or j) : 4. 1. 71 - 93

[1] Q1 - 4 = 'fathers', hence most modern texts set 'father's', Q5/Ff = 'Father'

[2] Qq and most modern texts = 'our', Q3 - 5/Ff = 'your'

[3] Q1 - 4 and most modern texts = 'a', Q5/Ff = 'the'

[4] though most modern texts follow a variant of Q1-2/Ff's 'shall o're-turne', Q3 - 5 offer the interesting 'shall, or turne'

[5] Q1-4/F4/most modern texts = 'as', F1 - 2 = 'At'

[6] Q1 - 4 and most modern texts = 'terme', Q5 = 'deame', Ff = 'Dreame'

LS [7] most modern texts follow Qq's regular setting of two pentameter lines, shown by the symbols °: Ff's irregular 4/11/5 syllables yet again sets up a somewhat incoherent style for the exuberant Scot

[8] most modern texts follow Q1 and add 'him', omitted by Q2 - 5/Ff

[9] Q1 - 2 and most modern texts = 'is', Q3 - 5/Ff = 'hath'

Hotspurre	He shall be welcome too. → [1]	
	Where is his Sonne,	
	The nimble-footed Mad-Cap, Prince of Wales,	
	And his Cumrades, that dast the World aside,	
110	And bid it passe?	

Vernon	All furnisht, all in Armes,
	All plum'd like Estridges, that with [2] the Winde
	Bayted like Eagles, having lately bath'd,
	Glittering in Golden Coates, like Images,
115	As full of spirit as the Moneth of May,
	And gorgeous as the Sunne at Mid-summer,
	Wanton as youthfull Goates, wilde as young Bulls.

I saw young Harry with his Bever on,
His Cushes on his thighes, gallantly arm'd,
120 Rise from the ground like *feathered Mercury,
And vaulted with such ease into his Seat,
As it an Angell dropt downe from the Clouds,
To turne and winde a fierie Pegasus,
And witch the World with Noble Horsemanship.

125 **Hotspurre** No more, no more, → [3]
Worse then the Sunne in March:
This prayse doth nourish Agues: let them come.

They come like Sacrifices in their trimme,
And to the fire-ey'd Maid of smoakie Warre,
130 All hot, and bleeding, will wee offer them:
The mayled Mars shall on his Altar [4] sit
Up to the eares in blood.
                              I am on fire,
To heare this rich reprizall is so nigh,
135 And yet not ours.
                      Come, let me take [5] my Horse,
Who is to beare me like a Thunder-bolt,
Against the bosome of the Prince of Wales.

R 66 - a (or j) : 4. 1. 94 - 121

SP [1]
most modern texts follow Qq and set Ff's two short lines as one line of verse: Ff's setting allows more of the moment for Hotspurre as he realises there may be a chance, at last, to face the Prince

▼ [2]
though some modern texts agree with Qq/Ff and print this as 'with', one splendid gloss = 'wing';
(commentators also suggest at least one following line might have been omitted by Qq/Ff)

SP [3]
again the two short lines as set in Ff are shown as one complete verse line in Qq and most modern texts: however, this does rob Hotspurre of the tiny moment in Ff as he seeks to dismiss the enormously unexpected positive response from his colleague about their/his adversary, the Prince of Wales

▼ [4]
Q1 - 2 = 'altars', Q3 - 5/Ff = 'Altar'

▼ [5]
Q1 and most modern texts = 'tast', Q3 - 5/Ff = 'take'

140		Harry to Harry, shall not Horse to Horse [1]
		Meete, and ne're part, till one drop downe a Coarse?
		Oh, that Glendower were come.
	Vernon	There is more newes :
		I learned in Worcester, as I rode along,
		He cannot draw his Power this foureteene dayes.
145	**Dowglas**	That's the worst Tidings that I heare of
		yet.
	Worcester	I by my faith, that beares a frosty sound.
	Hotspurre	What may the Kings whole Battaile reach
		unto?
150	**Vernon**	To thirty thousand.
	Hotspurre	Forty let it be,
		My Father and Glendower being both away,
		The powres of us, may serve so great a day.
155		Come, let us take a muster speedily :
		Doomesday is neere ; dye all, dye merrily.
	Dowglas	Talke not of dying, I am out of feare
		Of death, or deaths hand, for this one halfe yeare.

[Exeunt Omnes]

R 66 - a (or j)

R 66 - a (or j) : 4. 1. 122 - 136

[1] Q1 - 2 and most modern texts = 'to Harry shal hot horse . . .', Q3 - 5/Ff = 'to Harry, shall not Horse . . .'

Scæna Secunda

ENTER FALSTAFFE AND BARDOLPH

Falstaffe	Bardolph, get thee before to Coventry, fill me a Bottle of Sack, our Souldiers shall march through: wee'le to Sutton-cop-hill [1] to Night.
Bardolph	Will you give me Money, Captaine?
5 **Falstaffe**	Lay out, lay out.
Bardolph	This Bottle makes an Angell.
Falstaffe	And if it doe, take it for thy labour: and if it make twentie, take them all, Ile answere the Coynage. Bid my Lieutenant Peto meete me at the [2] Townes end.
10 **Bardolph**	I will Captaine: farewell.

[Exit]

Falstaffe	If I be not asham'd of my Souldiers, I am a sowc't-Gurnet: I have misus'd the Kings Presse damnably.
	I have got, in exchange of a hundred and fiftie
15	Souldiers, three hundred and odde Pounds.
	I presse me none but good House-holders, Yeomens sonnes: enquire me out contracted Batchelers, such as had beene ask'd twice on the Banes: such a Commoditie of warme slaves,
20	as had as lieve heare the Devill, as a Drumme; such as feare the report of a Caliver, worse then a struck-Foole,[3] or a hurt wilde-Ducke.
	I prest me none but such Tostes and Butter, with Hearts in their Bellyes no bigger then
25	Pinnesheads, and they have bought out their services: And now, my whole Charge consists of Ancients, Corporals, Lieutenants, Gentlemen of Companies, Slaves as

---

N 1 most modern texts set a more contemporary version of the place name, e.g. 'Sutton Co'fill' (i.e. 'Coalfield')

▼ 2 most modern texts follow Q1 - 4 and omit 'the' as set in Ff, Q5 = 'a'

▼ 3 most modern texts follow Q1 - 3 and keep the bird image of the next line by setting 'foule', Q4 - 5/Ff = 'Foole'

ragged as Lazarus in the painted Cloth, where the Glut-
tons Dogges licked his Sores; and such, as indeed were
30   never Souldiers, but dis-carded unjust Servingmen, younger Sonnes to younger Brothers, revolted Tapsters and
Ostlers, Trade-falne, the Cankers of a calme World, and [1]
long Peace, tenne times more dis-honorable ragged,
then an old-fac'd [2] Ancient; and such have I to fill up the
35   roomes of them that [3] have bought out their services: that
you would thinke, that I had a hundred and fiftie totter'd
Prodigalls, lately come from Swine-keeping, from eating
Draffe and Huskes.

                A mad fellow met me on the way,
40   and told me, I had unloaded all the Gibbets, and prest the
dead bodyes.

                   No eye hath seene such skar-Crowes: Ile
not march through Coventry with them, that's flat.

                                 Nay,
45   and the Villaines march wide betwixt the Legges, as if
they had Gyves on; for indeede, I had the most of them
out of Prison.

                  There's not a Shirt and a halfe in all my
Company: and the halfe Shirt is two Napkins tackt to-
50   gether, and throwne over shoulders like a Heralds
Coat, without sleeves: and the Shirt, to say the truth,
stolne from my Host of [4] S. [5] Albones, or the Red-Nose
Inne-keeper of Davintry.

                    But that's all one, they'le finde
55   Linnen enough on every Hedge.

ENTER THE PRINCE, AND THE LORD OF WESTMERLAND

Prince   How now blowne Jack? how now Quilt?

Falstaffe   What Hal?

                      How now mad Wag, what a Devill
do'st thou in Warwickshire?

60   My good Lord of Westmerland, I cry you mercy, I thought your Honour had already beene at Shrewsbury.

L 67 - a (or j) : 4. 2. 25 - 53

W [1] most modern texts follow Q1 - 4 and set 'a', omitted by Q5/Ff

W [2] most modern texts follow Q1 - 4 and set 'fazd', Q5 = 'faczde', Ff = 'fac'd': (the meaning is the same, no
matter which version is preferred)

W [3] Qq and most modern texts = 'as', Ff = 'that'

W [4] Q1 - 4 and most modern texts = 'at', Q5/Ff = 'of'

AB [5] 'S.' is the Ff equivalent of the modern 'St.' (for the word 'Saint')

Westmerland	'Faith, Sir John, 'tis more then time that I were	
	there, and you too : but my Powers are there alreadie.	
65	The King, I can tell you, lookes for us all : we must away	
	all to¹ Night.	L 67 - a (or j)
Falstaffe	Tut, never feare me, I am as vigilant as a Cat, to	
	steale Creame.	
Prince	I thinke to steale Creame indeed, for they theft	
70	hath alreadie made thee Butter : but tell me, Jack, whose	
	fellowes are these that come after?	
Falstaffe	Mine, Hal, mine.	
Prince	I did never see such pittifull Rascals.	
Falstaffe	Tut, tut, good enough to tosse : foode for Pow-	
75	der, foode for Powder : they'le fill a Pit, as well as better :	
	tush man, mortall men, mortall men.	
Westmerland	I, but Sir John, me thinkes they are exceeding	
	poore and bare, too beggarly.	
Falstaffe	Faith, for their povertie, I know not where they	
80	had that ; and for their barenesse, I am sure they never	
	learn'd that of me.	
Prince	No, Ile be sworne, unlesse you call three fingers	
	on ² the Ribbes bare.	
	But sirra, make haste, Percy is already	
85	in the field. ³	
Falstaffe	What, is the King encamp'd?	
Westmerland	Hee is, Sir John, I feare wee shall stay too	
	long. ⁴	
Falstaffe	Well,° to the latter end of a Fray, and the begin-	
90	ning of a Feast,° fits a dull fighter, and a keene Guest. ° ⁵	

[Exeunt]

L 67 - a (or j) / R 67 - a (or j) : 4. 2. 54 - 80

W ₁ most modern texts follow Qq and omit the 'to' as set by Ff: one gloss suggests substituting 'at'

W ₂ Q1 - 2 and most modern texts = 'in', Q3 - 5/Ff = 'on'

SD ₃ most modern texts follow Qq and set a stage direction here for the exit of the Prince

SD ₄ despite Qq/Ff's exeunt in two lines time, most modern texts add an exit here for Westmerland

LS ₅ though Qq/Ff set this as prose, most modern texts set the text in its couplet verse form, as shown

Scœna Tertia

ENTER HOTSPUR, WORCESTER, DOWGLAS, AND
VERNON

	Hotspurre	Wee'le fight with him to Night.
	Worcester	It may not be. }
	Dowglas	You give him then advantage.
	Vernon	Not a whit. }
5	**Hotspurre**	Why say you so? lookes he not for supply?
	Vernon	So doe wee.
	Hotspurre	His is certaine, ours is doubtfull. }
	Worcester	Good Cousin be advis'd, stirre not to night.
	Vernon	Doe not, my Lord.
10	**Dowglas**	You doe not counsaile well : } You speake it out of feare, and cold heart.
	Vernon	Doe me no slander, Dowglas : by my Life, And I dare well maintaine it with my Life, If well-respected Honor bid me on,
15		I hold as little counsaile with weake feare, As you, my Lord, or any Scot that this day lives.
		Let it be seene tomorrow in the Battell, Which of us feares.
	Dowglas	Yea, or to night. }
20	**Vernon**	Content. }
	Hotspurre	To night, say I.
	Vernon	Come, come, it may not be. }

I wonder much,° being më ¹ of such great leading as you are° ²
That you fore-see not what impediments
25   Drag backe our expedition :   certaine Horse
Of my Cousin Vernons are not yet come up,
Your Unckle Worcesters Horse ³ came but to day,
And now their pride and mettall is asleepe,
Their courage with hard labour tame and dull,
30   That not a Horse is halfe the halfe of ⁴ himselfe.

Hotspurre   So are the Horses of the Enemie
In generall journey bated, and brought low :
The better part of ours are full of rest.   R 67 - a (or j)

Worcester   The number of the King exceedeth ours :
35   For Gods sake, Cousin, stay till all come in.

**THE TRUMPET SOUNDS A PARLEY. ENTER SIR
WALTER BLUNT**

Blunt   I come with gracious offers from the King,
If you vouchsafe me hearing, and respect.

Hotspurre   Welcome, Sir Walter Blunt :
And would to God° you were of our determination. ° ⁵

40   Some of us love you well :   and even those some
Envie your great deservings, and good name,
Because you are not of our qualitie,
But stand against us like an Enemie.

Blunt   And 'Heaven defend, but still I should stand so,
45   So long as out of Limit, and true Rule,
You stand against anoynted Majestie.
But to my Charge. → ⁶
The King hath sent to know

R 67 - a (or j) / L 68 - a (or j) : 4. 3. 17 - 41

AB ¹ F1 - 2 = 'më', (printed as such because of lack of column width): Qq/F3/most modern texts = 'men'

LS ² though Qq/Ff set this as a 13 - 14 syllable line (perhaps suggesting Vernon is passionately moved by his argument), most modern texts remove his participation in the split verse line, thus creating a pause before he starts to speak, and then giving him two 'normal' lines (10 or 11/10 or 11 syllables) regularising the moment

W ³ some modern texts follow Q1 - 4 and set 'horses', Q5/Ff = 'Horse'

W ⁴ though Qq/Ff set 'half the halfe of', most modern texts omit 'of'

LS ⁵ Ff's irregular setting (6/13 or 14 syllables) allows for some sort of acknowledgment (an embrace?) between the first and long second line: most modern texts follow Qq's poetically correct setting (10/9 or 10) which removes the chance of physically establishing any feeling of respect from Hotspurre towards Blunt, a feeling which is later referred to by Hotspurre after Blunt's death, see page 108, line 130 this text

SP ⁶ most modern texts follow Qq and set the two short Ff lines as a complete verse line: the Ff setting allows Blunt a brief moment as he changes from voicing his own opinions to acting as the King's messenger

The nature of your Griefes, and whereupon
50   You conjure from the Brest of Civill Peace,
Such bold Hostilitie, teaching his dutious Land
Audacious Crueltie.
                    If that the King
Have any way your good Deserts forgot,
55   Which he confesseth to be manifold,
He bids you name your Griefes, and with all speed
You shall have your desires, with interest;
And Pardon absolute for your selfe, and these,
Herein mis-led, by your suggestion.

60 **Hotspurre**   The King is kinde: → [1]
All well wee know, the King
Knowes at what time to promise, when to pay.

My Father, [2] my Unckle, and my selfe,
Did give him that same Royaltie he weares:
65   And when he was not sixe and twentie strong,
Sicke in the Worlds regard, wretched, and low,
A poore unminded Out-law, sneaking home,
My Father gave him welcome to the shore:
And when he heard him sweare, and vow to God,
70   He came but to be Duke of Lancaster,
To sue his Liverie, and begge his Peace,
With teares of Innocencie, and tearmes of Zeale;
My Father, in kinde heart and pitty mov'd,
Swore him assistance, and perform'd it too.

75   Now, when the Lords and Barons of the Realme
Perceiv'd Northumberland did leane to him,
The more and lesse came in with Cap and Knee,
Met him in Boroughs, Cities, Villages,
Attended him on Bridges, stood in Lanes,
80   Layd Gifts before him, proffer'd him their Oathes,
Gave him their Heires, [3] as Pages followed him,
Even at the heeles, in golden mutltitudes.

He presently, as Greatnesse knowes it selfe,
Steps me a little higher then his Vow
85   Made to my Father, while his blood was poore,
Upon the naked shore at Ravenspurgh:

L 68 - a (or j) : 4. 3. 42 - 77

SP [1]
most modern texts follow Qq and set the two short Ff lines as a complete verse line: however, the Ff setting
allows Hotspurre a silent moment as he attempts to give Blunt a (expletive deleted?) reply

W [2]
modern texts follow Q1 - 2 and set 'and', omitted by Q3 - 5/Ff

PCT [3]
though Qq/F1 - 3 set 'heires, as Pages', some modern texts follow F4 in repositioning the comma, thus
substantially altering the meaning, viz. 'heirs as pages,'

90	And now (forsooth) takes on him to reforme Some certaine Edicts, and some strait Decrees, That lay [1] too heavie on the Common-wealth; Cryes out upon abuses, seemes to weepe Over his Countries Wrongs: and by this Face, This seeming Brow of Justice, did he winne The hearts of all that hee did angle for.

Proceede further, cut me off the Heads
95   Of all the Favorites, that the absent King
In deputation left behind him heere,   L 68 - a (or j)
When hee was personall in the Irish Warre.

Blunt   Tut, I came not to heare this.

Hotspurre   Then to the point.   )

100   In short time after, hee depos'd the King.

Soone after that, depriv'd him of his Life:
And in the neck of that, task't the whole State.

To make that worse, suffer'd his Kinsman March,
Who is, if every Owner were [2] plac'd,
105   Indeede his King, to be engag'd in Wales,
There, without Ransome, to lye forfeited:
Disgrac'd me in my happie Victories,
Sought to intrap me by intelligence,
Rated 'my Unckle from the Councell-Boord,
110   In rage dismis'd my Father from the Court,
Broke Oath on Oath, committed Wrong on Wrong,
And in conclusion, drove us to seeke out
This Head of safetie; and withall, to prie
Into his Title: [3] the which wee finde
115   Too indirect, for long continuance.

Blunt   Shall I returne this answer to the King?

Hotspurre   Not so, Sir Walter. → [4]

Wee'le with-draw a while:
Goe to the King, and let there be impawn'd
120   Some suretie for a safe returne againe,

L 68 - a (or j) / R 68 - a (or j) :   4. 3. 78 - 109

▼ [1]   Q1 - 4 and most modern texts = 'lie', Q5/Ff = 'lay'

▼ [2]   most modern texts follow Q1 - 4 = 'were well plac'd', Q5/ F1 - 2 = 'were plac'd', F3 - 4 = 'were right plac'd'

▼ [3]   as Qq/Ff set a nine syllable line, some modern texts add 'too' to maintain the pentameter

SP [4]   again, at a key point between the two men, most modern texts follow Qq and set Ff's two short lines as a complete verse line: the Ff setting allows Hotspurre a brief pause to assess Blunt's response before modifying his stance

	And in the Morning early shall *my Unckle
	Bring him our purpose: ¹ and so farewell.
Blunt	I would you would accept of Grace and Love.
Hotspurre	And't ² may be, so wee shall.
Blunt	Pray *Heaven you doe.

125 at left beside **Blunt** row.

[Exeunt]

R 68 - a (or j) : 4. 3. 110 - 113

▼ ₁ most modern texts follow Q1 - 3 and set 'purposes', Q5/Ff = 'purpose'
▼ ₂ Qq and most modern texts = 'And', Ff = 'And't'

Scena Quarta

ENTER THE ARCH-BISHOP OF YORKE, AND SIR MICHELL

Archbishop	Hie, good Sir Michell, beare this sealed Briefe	
	With winged haste to the Lord Marshall,	
	This to my Cousin Scroope, and all the rest	

To whom they are directed.

5   If you knew° how much they doe import,
You would make haste. °

Sir Michell   My good Lord,° I guesse their tenor.

Archbishop   Like enough you doe. ° ¹

To morrow, good Sir Michell, is a day,
10   Wherein the fortune of ten thousand men
Must bide the touch.
           For Sir, at Shrewsbury,
As I am truly given to understand,
The King, with mightie and quick-raysed Power,
15   Meetes with Lord Harry: and I feare, Sir Michell,
What with the sicknesse of Northumberland,
Whose Power was in the first proportion;
And what with Owen Glendowers absence thence,
Who with them was rated firmely ² too,
20   And comes not in, over-rul'd by Prophecies,
I feare the Power of Percy is too weake,
To wage in instant tryall with the King.

Sir Michell   Why, my good Lord, you need not feare,
There is Dowglas, and Lord Mortimer.

25   **Archbishop**   No, Mortimer is not there.

ᴸˢ ₁ most modern texts follow Qq's almost regular setting of the passage as shown by the symbols ° (10/10 /3/10 syllables): Ff are alone in setting the tiny hesitations for both Sir Michell and the Archbishop as they avoid direct mention of the words 'treachery' or 'treason' (7/9/4/8/5 syllables)

ᵂ ₂ Q1 = 'was a rated sinew too', Q4 = 'rated sinew', Q5/Ff = 'was rated firmely too'

Sir Michell	But there is Mordake, Vernon, Lord Harry Percy,

And there is my Lord of Worcester,
And a Head° of gallant Warriors,
Noble Gentlemen. ° [1]   R 68 - a (or j)

30 **Archbishop**	And so there is, but yet the King hath drawne
	The speciall head of all the Land together:
	The Prince of Wales, Lord John of Lancaster,
	The Noble Westmerland, and warlike Blunt;
	And many moe Corrivals, and deare men
35	Of estimation, and command in Armes.
Sir Michell	Doubt not my Lord, he [2] shall be well oppos'd [3]
Archbishop	I hope no lesse?
	Yet needfull 'tis to feare,
	And to prevent the worst, Sir Michell speed;
40	For if Lord Percy thrive not, ere the King
	Dismisse his power, he meanes to visit us:
	For he hath heard of our Confederacie,
	And, 'tis but Wisedome to make strong against him:
	Therefore make hast, I must go write againe
45	To other Friends: and so farewell, Sir Michell.

[Exeunt]

R 68 - a (or j) / L 69 - b : 4. 4. 24 - 41

LS [1] most modern texts follow Qq and set an almost 'regular' passage (11/10 or 11 syllables): Ff allow more
breathless moments for Sir Michell's counter-argument to the news of Mortimer's absence (8/8 or 9/5 syllables)

W [2] most modern texts follow Q1 - 3 and set 'they', Q4 - 5/Ff = 'he'

PCT [3] F1 is the only text that sets no punctuation at the end of the speech - probably because of lack of sufficient
column width: (if this were not so, the lack of punctuation might suggest that the Archbishop interrupts Sir
Michell): Qq/F2 and most modern texts set a period

Actus Quintus. Scena Prima

**ENTER THE KING, PRINCE OF WALES, LORD JOHN OF LANCASTER,
EARLE OF WESTMERLAND, SIR WALTER BLUNT,
AND FALSTAFFE**

King   How bloodily the Sunne beings to peere
Above yon busky [1] hill : the day lookes pale
At his distemperature.

Prince   The Southerne winde
5   Doth play the Trumpet to his purposes,
And by his hollow whistling in the Leaves,
Fortels a Tempest, and a blust'ring day.

King   Then with the losers let it sympathize,
For nothing can seeme foule to those that win.

[The Trumpet sounds]
ENTER WORCESTER

10   **King**   How now my Lord of Worster?
'Tis not well
That you and I should meet upon such tearmes,
As now we meet.
You have deceiv'd our trust,
15   And made us doffe our easie Robes of Peace,
To crush our old limbes in ungentle Steele :
This is not well, my Lord, this is not well.

What say you to it? will you againe unknit
This churlish knot of all-abhorred Warre?
20   And move in that obedient Orbe againe,
Where you did give a faire and naturall light,
And be no more an exhall'd Meteor,
A prodigie of Feare, and a Portent
Of broached Mischeefe, to the unborne Times?

25   **Worcester**   Heare me, my Liege :
For mine owne part, I could be well content
To entertaine the Lagge-end of my life
With quiet houres : For I do [2] protest,

---

[1] Q2 - 5/Ff/most modern texts = 'busky' (i.e. 'bosky' or 'wooded'): hardly any modern text sets Q1's 'bulky'

[2] most modern texts follow Qq and set 'I', Ff = 'I do'

		I have not sought the day of this dislike.
30	**King**	You have not sought it: how comes it then?
	Falstaffe	Rebellion lay in his way, and he found it.
	Prince	Peace, Chewet, peace.
	Worcester	It pleas'd your Majesty, to turne your lookes
		Of Favour, from my Selfe, and all our House;
35		And yet I must remember you my Lord,
		We were the first, and dearest of your Friends:
		For you, my staffe of Office did I breake
		In Richards time, and poasted day and night
		To meete you on the way, and kisse your hand,
40		When yet you were in place, and in account
		Nothing so strong and fortunate, as I;
		It was my Selfe, my Brother, and his Sonne,
		That brought you home, and boldly did out-dare
		The danger ¹ of the time.
45		You swore to us,
		And you did sweare that Oath at Doncaster,
		That you did nothing of ² purpose 'gainst the State,
		Nor claime no further, then your new-falne right,
		The seate of Gaunt, Dukedome of Lancaster,
50		To this, we sware ³ our aide: But in short space,
		It rain'd downe Fortune showring on your head,
		And such a floud of Greatnesse fell on you,
		What with our helpe, what with the absent King,
		What with the injuries of ⁴ wanton time,
55		The seeming sufferances that you had borne,
		And the contrarious Windes that held the King
		So long in the ⁵ unlucky Irish Warres,
		That all in England did repute him dead:
		And from this swarme of faire advantages,
60		You tooke occasion to be quickly woo'd,
		To gripe the generall sway into your hand,
		Forgot your Oath to us at Doncaster,
		And being fed by us, you us'd us so,
		As that ungentle gull the Cuckowes Bird,
65		Useth the Sparrow, did oppresse our Nest,

L 69 - b

L 69 - b / R 69 - b : 5. 1. 26 - 61

▼ ¹ most modern texts follow Q1 - 4 and set 'dangers', Q5/Ff = 'danger'

▼ ² most modern texts follow Q1 - 4 and set 'nothing purpose', Q5/Ff = 'nothing of purpose'

▼ ³ Q1 - 4 = 'swore', Q5 = 'sweare', Ff = 'sware'

▼ ⁴ most modern texts follow Q1 - 4 and set 'of a', Q5/Ff = 'of'

▼ ⁵ most modern texts follow Q1 - 4 and set 'his', Q5/Ff = 'the'

Grew by our Feeding, to so great a bulke,
That even our Love durst not come neere your sight
For feare of swallowing : But with nimble wing
We were inforc'd for safety sake, to flye
70   Out of your sight, and raise this present Head,
Whereby we stand opposed by such meanes
As you your selfe, have forg'd against your selfe,
By unkinde usage, dangerous countenance,
And violation of all faith and troth
75   Sworne to us in [1] yonger enterprize.

King   These things indeede you have articulated,[2]
Proclaim'd at Market Crosses, read in Churches,
To face the Garment of Rebellion
With some fine colour, that may please the eye
80   Of fickle Changelings, and poore Discontents,
Which gape, and rub the Elbow at the newes
Of hurly burly Innovation :
And never yet did Insurrection want
Such water-colours, to impaint his cause :
85   Nor moody Beggars, starving for a time
Of pell-mell havocke, and confusion.

Prince   In both our[3] Armies, there is many a soule
Shall pay full dearely for this encounter,
If once they joyne in triall.
90   Tell your Nephew,
The Prince of Wales doth joyne with all the world
In praise of Henry Percie : By my Hopes,
This present enterprize set off his head,
I do not thinke a braver Gentleman,
95   More active, valiant, or more valiant yong,
More daring, or more bold, is now alive,
To grace this latter Age with Noble deeds.

For my part, I may speake it to my shame,
I have a Truant beene to Chivalry,
100   And so I heare, he doth account me too :
Yet this before my Fathers Majesty,
I am content that he shall take the oddes
Of his great name and estimation,
And will, to save the blood on either side,
105   Try fortune with him, in a Single Fight.

---

[1] most modern texts follow Qq/F3 and set 'your', omitted by F1 - 2

[2] Qq and most modern texts = 'articulate', Ff = 'articulated'

[3] Qq and some modern texts = 'your', Ff = 'our'

King	And Prince of Wales, so dare we venter thee,	
	Albeit, consideration infinite	R 69 - b
	Do make against it : No good Worster, no,	
	We love our people well ; even those we love	
110	That are misled upon your Cousins part :	
	And will they take the offer of our Grace :	
	Both he, and they, and you ; yea, every man	
	Shall be my Friend againe, and Ile be his.	

	So tell your Cousin, and bring me word,
115	What he will do.
	But if he will not yeeld,
	Rebuke and dread correction waite on us,
	And they shall do their Office.
	So bee gone,
120	We will not now be troubled with reply,
	We offer faire, take it advisedly.

EXIT WORCESTER [1]

Prince	It will not be accepted, on my life,
	The Dowglas and the Hotspurre both together,
	Are confident against the world in Armes.

125 **King**	Hence therefore, every Leader to his charge,
	For on their answer will we set on them ;
	And God befriend us, as our cause is just.

[Exeunt]
MANET PRINCE AND FALSTAFFE

Falstaffe	[2]	Hal, if thou see me downe in the battell,
		And bestride me, so ; 'tis a point of friendship.
130 **Prince**		Nothing but a Colosssus can do thee that frendship [3]
		Say thy prayers, and farewell.
Falstaffe		I would *it were bed time Hal, and all well.

Prince	Why, thou ow'st *heaven a death.

R 69 - b / L 70 - b : 5. 1. 101 - 126

UE/SD [1] this is probably one of the more noticeable exits in the play since it is set on a separate line rather than alongside the text, suggesting the exit stops all on-stage action until completed: also, most modern texts add Vernon to the exit

LS/VP [2] Qq/Ff set in verse the opening of this serious interchange by Falstaffe (10/11 syllables) and the teasing reply of the Prince (13/7): this allows greater weight for the moment for the text to switch into the less formal prose, especially with Falstaffe's soliloquy: sadly, most modern texts set the complete sequence as prose

PCT [3] F1 sets no punctuation, probably through lack of column width: F2/most modern texts set a semi-colon, Qq a comma

Falstaffe ¹ 'Tis not due yet : I would bee loath to pay him
before his day.
What neede I bee so forward with him,
that call's not on me?
Well, 'tis no matter, Honor prickes
me on.
² But how if Honour pricke me off when I come
on?
How then?
Can Honour set too a legge?
No : or an
arme?
No : Or take away the greefe of a wound?
No.
Honour hath no skill in Surgerie, then?
No.
What is Ho-
nour?
A word.
What is that word Honour?
Ayre : A
trim reckoning.
Who hath it?
He that dy'de a Wednes-
day.
Doth he feele it?
No.
Doth hee heare it?
No.
³ Is it
insensible then? yea, to the dead.
But wil it not live with
the living?
No.
Why?
Detraction will not suffer it, ther-
fore Ile none of it.
Honour is a meere Scutcheon, and so
ends my Catechisime. †⁴

[Exit]

L 70 - b : 5. 1. 127 - 141

ˢᴰ ¹ the word 'exit' is set at the end of Falstaffe's speech suggesting that it is a soliloquy: though not indicated in
Qq/Ff, most modern texts have the Prince exit before Falstaffe begins his speech: however, it could occur after the
first phrase, or even at the end of the first sentence

ᵂ ² most modern texts follow Qq and set 'yea', which Ff omit

ᵂ³ most modern texts follow Qq and set 'tis', Ff = 'Is it'

ᵂ⁴ F1 = 'Catechisne', F2/most modern texts = 'Catechisme'

Scena Secunda

ENTER WORCESTER, AND SIR RICHARD VERNON

Worcester	O no, my Nephew must not know, Sir Richard,
	The liberall kinde[1] offer of the King.
Vernon	'Twere best he did.
Worcester	Then we are[2] all undone.

5
     It is not possible, it cannot be,
     The King would[3] keepe his word in loving us,
     He will suspect us still, and finde a time
     To punish this offence in others[4] faults:
     Supposition,[5] all our lives, shall be stucke full of eyes;
10
     For Treason is but trusted like the Foxe,
     Who 'ne're so tame, so cherisht, and lock'd up,
     Will have a wilde tricke of his Ancestors:
     Looke how he[6] can, or sad or merrily,
     Interpretation will misquote our lookes,
15
     And we shall feede like Oxen at a stall,
     The better cherisht, still the nearer death.

     My Nephewes trespasse may be well forgot,
     It hath the excuse of youth, and heate of blood,   L 70 - b
     And an adopted name of Priviledge,†[7]
20
     A haire-brain'd Hotspurre, govern'd by a Spleene:
     All his offences live upon my head,
     And on his Fathers.
                We did traine him on,
     And his corruption being tane from us,
25
     We as the Spring of all, shall pay for all:
     Therefore good Cousin, let not Harry know
     In any case, the offer of the King.

L 70 - b / R 70 - b : 5. 2. 1 - 25

[1] Q1 and some modern texts = 'and kinde', Q2 - 5/Ff = 'kinde'

[2] Qq and most modern texts = 'are we', Ff = 'we are'

[3] Q1 - 3 = 'should', Q4 - 5/Ff = 'would'

[4] Q1 - 4 and most modern texts = 'other', Ff = 'others'

[5] Qq/Ff most modern texts = 'Supposition', one commentator suggests 'Suspicion'

[6] Q1 - 3/F3 and most modern texts = 'we', Q4 - 5/F1 - 2 = 'he'

[7] F1 = 'Ptiviledge', F2/most modern texts = 'Priviledge'

	Vernon	Deliver what you will, Ile say 'tis so. Heere comes your Cosin.

ENTER HOTSPURRE [1]

30	**Hotspurre**	My Unkle is return'd, Deliver up my Lord of Westmerland. Unkle, what newe-? [2]
	Worcester	The King will bid you battell presently.
	Dowglas	Defie him by the Lord of Westmerland.
35	**Hotspurre**	Lord Dowglas : Go you and tell him so :
	Dowglas	Marry and shall, and verie willingly.

[Exit Dowglas]

	Worcester	There is no seeming mercy in the King.
	Hotspurre	Did you begge any? God forbid.
40	**Worcester**	I told him gently of our greevances, Of his Oath-breaking : which he mended thus, By now forswearing that he is forsworne, He cals us Rebels, Traitors, and will scourge With haughty armes, this hatefull name in us.

ENTER DOWGLAS

45	**Dowglas**	Arme Gentlemen, to Armes, for I have thrown A brave defiance in King Henries teeth : And Westmerland that was ingag'd did beare it, Which cannot choose but bring him quickly on.
50	**Worcester**	The Prince of Wales stept forth before the king, And Nephew, challeng'd you to single fight.

55	**Hotspurre**	O, would the quarrell lay upon our heads,
		And that no man might draw short breath to day,
		But I and Harry Monmouth.
		                  Tell me, tell mee,
		How shew'd his Talking? [3]
		                       Seem'd it in contempt?

---

[1] most modern texts add Dowglas to the entry

[2] Qq/F2 and most modern texts = 'newes', F1 = 'newe-'

[3] Q1 and some modern texts = 'tasking', Q2 - 5/Ff = 'Talking'

Vernon	No, by my Soule : I never in my life
	Did heare a Challenge urg'd more modestly,
	Unlesse a Brother should a Brother dare
60	To gentle exercise, and proofe of Armes.
	He gave you all the Duties of a Man,
	Trimm'd up your praises with a Princely tongue,
	Spoke your deservings like a Chronicle,
	Making you ever better then his praise,
65	By still dispraising praise, valew'd with you :
	And which became him like a Prince indeed,
	He made a blushing citall of himselfe,
	And chid his Trewant youth with such a Grace,
	As if he mastred there a double spirit
70	Of teaching, and of learning instantly :
	There did he pause.

He gave you all the Duties of a Man,
Trimm'd up your praises with a Princely tongue,
Spoke your deservings like a Chronicle,
Making you ever better then his praise,
By still dispraising praise, valew'd with you :
And which became him like a Prince indeed,
He made a blushing citall of himselfe,
And chid his Trewant youth with such a Grace,
As if he mastred there a double spirit
Of teaching, and of learning instantly :
There did he pause.
                              But let me tell the World,
If he out-live the envie of this day,
England did never owe so sweet a hope,
So much misconstrued in his Wantonnesse.

Hotspurre   Cousin, I thinke thou art enamored
On his Follies : never did I heare
Of any Prince so wilde at Liberty. [1]

But be he as he will, yet once ere night,
I will imbrace him with a Souldiers arme,
That he shall shrinke under my curtesie.

Arme, arme with speed.
                              And Fellow's, [2] Soldiers, Friends,
Better consider what you have to do,
That [3] I that have not well the gift of Tongue,   R 70 - b
Can lift your blood up with perswasion.

ENTER A MESSENGER

Messenger   My Lord, heere are Letters for you.

Hotspurre   I cannot reade them now.

O Gentlemen[†4], the time of life is short ;
To spend that shortnesse basely, were too long.

R 70 - b / L 71 - b : 5. 2. 51 - 82

[w1] Q1 - 4 = 'a libertie', Q5/Ff = 'at Liberty', one good modern gloss = 'a libertine'

[w2] Q1 - 4/F4/most modern texts = 'fellowes', F1 - 3 = Fellow's'

[w3] Q1-2/F2 and most modern texts = 'Then', Q3 - 5/F1 = 'That'

[w4] F1 = 'OGentlemen', F2 = 'O Gentlemen'

If life did ride upon a Dials point,
Still ending at the arrivall of an houre,
And if we live, we live to treade on Kings:
If dye; brave death, when Princes dye with us.

95 Now for our Consciences, the Armes is [1] faire,
When the intent for bearing them is just.

ENTER ANOTHER MESSENGER

Messenger   My Lord prepare, the King comes on apace.

Hotspurre   I thanke him, that he cuts me from my tale:
For I professe not talking: Onely this,

100
> Let each man do his best.
>   And heere I draw° [2] a Sword,
> Whose worthy [3] temper I intend to staine° [4]

With the best blood that I can meete withall,
In the adventure of this perillous day.

105 Now Esperance Percy, and set on:
Sound all the lofty Instruments of Warre,
And by that Musicke, let us all imbrace:
For heaven to earth, some of us never shall,
A second time do such a curtesie.

**THEY EMBRACE, THE TRUMPETS SOUND, THE KING ENTERETH
WITH HIS POWER, ALARUM UNTO THE BATTELL. THEN ENTER
DOWGLAS, AND SIR WALTER BLUNT [5]**
[Most modern texts create a new scene here, Act Five Scene 3]

110
> Blunt   What is thy name, that in [6] battel thus° ÿ [7] crossest me?
> What honor dost thou seeke° upon my head?
>
> Dowglas   Know then my name is Dowglas,° [8]

And I do haunt thee in the battell thus,
Because some tell me, that thou art a King.

L 71 - b : 5. 2. 83 - 5. 3. 5

W [1] Q1 - 4 and most modern texts = 'are', Q5/Ff = 'is'

W [2] Ff = 'I draw', Qq/most modern texts = 'draw I'

W [3] Ff set 'worthy', Qq/some modern texts do not set the word

LS [4] however these two lines are going to be set, there has to be some irregularity: Ff put the long 12 syllable
line first, placing the emphasis on Hotspurre's production of his sword: Qq and most modern texts place it
second, thus putting the emphasis on the idea of drawing blood

SD [5] most modern texts add that Blunt is in the clothes of/disguised as the King

W [6] most modern texts add 'the' to turn the newly created line into pentameter

AB [7] F1 - 2 = 'ÿ', (printed as such because of lack of column width), F3/most modern texts = 'thou'

LS [8] the Qq/Ff irregular setting (13/10/7 syllables) allows the first moment of heat to be quickly controlled as the
seriousness of the situation settles in: the modern restructuring (11 - with 'the'/10/11) is simply too polite

115	**Blunt**	They tell theé true.
	Dowglas	The Lord of Stafford deere to day hath bought Thy likenesse : for insted of thee King Harry, This Sword hath ended him, so shall it thee, Unlesse thou yeeld thee as a [1] Prisoner.
120	**Blunt**	I was not borne to yeeld, thou haughty [2] Scot, And thou shalt finde a King that will revenge Lord [†3] Staffords death.

FIGHT, BLUNT IS SLAINE, THEN ENTERS HOTSPUR

	Hotspurre	O Dowglas, had'st thou fought at Holmedon thus I never had triumphed o're [4] a Scot.
125	**Dowglas**	All's done, all's won, here breathles lies the king
	Hotspurre	Where?
	Dowglas	Heere.
	Hotspurre	This Dowglas? No, I know this face full well :
130		A gallant Knight he was, his name was Blunt, Semblably furnish'd like the King himselfe.
	Dowglas	Ah foole : go [5] with thy soule whether it goes, A borrowed Title hast thou bought too deere. Why did'st thou tell me, that thou wer't a King?
135	**Hotspurre**	The King hath many marching in his Coats.
	Dowglas	Now by my Sword, I will kill all his Coates, Ile murder all his Wardrobe peece by peece, Until I meet the King. }
	Hotspurre	Up, and away,
140		Our Souldiers stand full fairely for the day.

[Exeunt]

ALARUM, AND ENTER FALSTAFFE SOLUS

▼ [1] most modern texts follow Q1 - 4 and set 'my', Q5/Ff = 'a'

▼ [2] Q1 - 4 and most modern texts = 'a yeelder thou proud', Q5 = 'to yeeld, thou proud', Ff = 'to yeeld, thou haughty'

▼ [3] Qq/F2/most modern texts = 'Lord', F1 = 'Lords'

▼ [4] Q1 - 2 = 'triumpht upon', Q3 - 5 = 'triumpht over', Ff = 'triumphed o're'

▼ [5] though Qq = 'Ah foole, goe', and Ff = 'Ah foole: go', most modern texts set the much weaker 'A fool go'

Falstaffe	Though I could scape shot-free at London, I feare
	the shot heere: here's no scoring, but upon the pate.

                                             Soft

who are you?

145   Sir Walter Blunt, there's Honour for you:

here's no vanity, I am as hot as molten Lead, and as heavy too; *heaven keepe Lead out of mee, I neede no more
weight then mine owne Bowelles.

                                I have led my rag of   L 71-b

150 Muffins ¹ where they are peppr'd: there's not three of my
150. left alive, and they ² for the Townes end, to beg during life.

        But who comes heere.

ENTER THE PRINCE

Prince	What, stand'st ³ thou idle heere?

155   Lend me thy sword,
Many a Nobleman likes ⁴ starke and stiffe
Under the hooves of vaunting enemies,
   ⁵ Whose deaths are ⁶ unreveng'd.
                  ⁷ Prethy lend me thy sword ⁸

160 **Falstaffe**	O Hal, I prethee give me leave to breath a while:
	Turke Gregory never did such deeds in Armes, as I have
	done this day.

        I have paid Percy, I have made him sure.

Prince	He is indeed, and living to kill thee:
165	I prethee lend me thy sword.

Falstaffe	Nay ⁹ Hal, if Percy bee alive, thou getst ¹⁰ not my
	Sword; but take my Pistoll if thou wilt.

L 71 - b / R 71 - b : 5. 3. 30 - 51

¹ Qq/Ff = 'rag of Muffins', most modern texts = 'ragamuffins'

² Qq/most modern texts set 'are', Ff omit the word

³ Q1 and most modern texts = 'stands', Q2 - 5/Ff = 'stand'st'

⁴ Qq/F2 and most modern texts = 'lies', F1 = 'likes'

⁵ some modern texts follow Q1 and set this final line as prose: however, at least one modern text startlingly sets the remainder of the scene until the Prince's exit as verse (a style never shared between the Prince and Falstaffe throughout the play so far)

⁶ most modern texts set Qq's 'yet' (or expand it to 'as yet'), which Ff omit

⁷ most modern texts follow Qq and add 'I', which Ff omit

⁸ F1 - 3 set no punctuation, probably because of too little column width: if it were intentional it might suggest that Falstaffe interrupts him: F4/Qq and most modern texts print a period

⁹ most modern texts follow Qq and set the oath omitted by Ff, 'before God'

¹⁰ Qq and most modern texts = 'gets', Q2 - 5/Ff = 'getst'

Prince	Give it me: What, is it in the Cafe?
Falstaffe	I Hal, 'tis hot: [1] There's that will Sacke a City.

THE PRINCE DRAWES OUT A BOTTLE OF SACKE

170   **Prince**   What, is it a time to jest and dally now.

[Exit]
[Throwes it at him]

Falstaffe   [2] If Percy be alive, Ile pierce him: if he do come in
my way, so: if he do not, if I come in his (willingly) let
him make a Carbonado for me: I like not such grinning
honour as Sir Walter hath: Give mee life, which if I can
175   save, so: if not, honour comes unlook'd for, and ther's an
end.

[Exit]

▼ [1] most modern texts follow Q1 - 4 and repeat "tis hot'; the repetition is omitted by Ff

▼ [2] most modern texts follow Q1 - 4 and add 'Well', omitted by Ff

Scena Tertia

[because of the earlier alteration, most modern texts list the new scene as #4]

ALARUM, EXCURSIONS, ENTER THE KING, THE PRINCE,
LORD JOHN OF LANCASTER, AND EARLE
OF WESTMERLAND

King	I prethee° Harry withdraw thy selfe, thou *blee- dest too much: ° Lord John of Lancaster, go you with him. ° 1	
Prince John	Not I, my Lord, unlesse I did bleed too.	
5	**Prince**	I beseech your Majsty make up, Least you ² retirement do amaze your friends.
	King	I will do so: My Lord of Westmerland° leade him to his Tent. ° 3
	Westmerland	Come my Lord, Ile leade you to your Tent.
10	**Prince**	Lead me my Lord? I do not need your helpe; And *heaven forbid a shallow scratch should drive The Prince of Wales from such a field as this, Where stain'd Nobility lyes troden on, And Rebels Armes triumph in massacres.
15	**Prince John as** **John**	We breath too long: Come cosin Westmerland, Our duty this way lies, for *heavens sake come. ⁴
20	**Prince**	By *heaven thou hast deceiv'd me Lancaster, I did not thinke thee Lord of such a spirit: Before, I lov'd thee as a Brother, John; But now, I do respect thee as my Soule.

^{VP}¹ most modern texts follow Q1 and set the opening in verse: Q2 - 5/Ff set it as prose, as if perhaps the immediacy of the battle is still being felt by the King

^W² Qq/F3/most modern texts = 'your', F1 - 2 = 'you'

^{LS}³ because of its length, this speech has to be set irregularly: Qq set the whole as one line: Ff set it as 4/11 syllables, with the pause allowing for a possible moment of physical weakness from the Prince prompting the King's concern: most modern texts set it as 10/5, with whatever physical moment there might be coming after the speech is complete

^{SD}⁴ most modern texts add a stage direction here for the exit of Prince John and Westmerland

King	I saw him hold Lord Percy at the point,
	With lustier maintenance then I did looke for

Of such an ungrowne Warriour.

| Prince | O this Boy,[1] lends mettal to us all. |

[Exit]
ENTER DOWGLAS

25   **Dowglas**   Another King?
          They grow like Hydra's heads:
I am the Dowglas, fatall to all those
That weare those colours on them.
          What art thou
30   That counterfeit'st the person of a King?

King   The King himselfe: who Dowglas grieves at hart   R 71 - b
So many of his shadowes thou hast met,
And not the very King.
          I have two Boyes
35   Seeke Percy and thy selfe about the Field:
But seeing thou fall'st on me so luckily,
I will assay thee: so[2] defend thy selfe.

Dowglas   I feare thou art another counterfeit:
And yet infaith thou ˙bear'st thee like a King:
40   But mine I am sure thou art, whoere thou be,
And thus I win thee.

[They fight, the K .{ing} being in danger]
ENTER PRINCE

Prince   Hold up they[3] head vile Scot, or thou art like
Never to hold it up againe: the Spirits
Of valiant Sherly, Stafford, Blunt, are in my Armes;
45   It is the Prince of Wales that threatens thee,
Who never promiseth, but he meanes to pay.

[They fight, Dowglas flyeth]

Cheerely My Lord: how fare's your Grace?

R 71 - b / L 72 - b : 5. 4. 21 - 44

[LS] [1] though this is as set in Qq/Ff, most modern texts add the phrase 'O this Boy' to the previous line, thus creating a normal line followed by a short one (10/6 syllables): however, the Qq/Ff irregularity (7/9 syllables) allows a moment of shared silence between father and son as they contemplate (and perhaps draw strength from) the valiant actions of the younger brother

[W] [2] Qq and most modern texts = 'and', Ff = 'so'

[W] [3] Qq/F2 and most modern texts = 'thy', F1 = 'they'

		Sir Nicholas Gawsey hath for succor sent,
		And so hath Clifton : Ile to Clifton straight.
50	**King**	Stay, and breath awhile.

Thou hast redeem'd thy lost opinion,
And shew'd thou mak'st some tender of my life
In this faire rescue thou hast brought to mee.

Prince   O °heaven, they did me too much injury,
55   That ever said I hearkned to [1] your death.

If it were so, I might have let alone
The insulting hand of Dowglas over you,
Which would have bene as speedy in your end,
As all the poysonous Potions in the world,
60   And sav'd the Treacherous labour of your Sonne.

King   Make up to Clifton, Ile to Sir Nicholas Gausey.

[Exit]
ENTER HOTSPUR

Hotspurre   If I mistake not, thou art Harry Monmouth.

Prince   Thou speak'st as if I would deny my name.

Hotspurre	My name is Harrie Percie.
65 **Prince**	Why then I see° a very valiant rebel of that [2] name. ° [3]

I am the Prince of Wales, and thinke not Percy,
To share with me in glory any more :
Two Starres keepe not their motion in one Sphere,
Nor can one England brooke a double reigne,
70   Of Harry Percy, and the Prince of Wales.

Hotspurre   Nor [4] shall it Harry, for the houre is come
To end the one of us ; and would to °heaven,
Thy name in Armes, were now as great as mine.

Prince   Ile make it greater, ere I part from thee,
75   And all the budding Honors of thy Crest,
Ile crop, to make a Garland for my head.

L 72 - b   :   5. 4. 45 - 73

▼ [1] Q1 - 3 and most modern texts = 'for', Q4 - 5/Ff = 'to'

▼ [2] most modern texts follow Q1 - 2 and set 'the', Q3 - 5/Ff = 'that'

LS [3] though the Qq/Ff irregularity (7/14 syllables) heightens the long-awaited for climax to the play, and allows
for a splendid acknowledgment between them, most modern texts readjust the text to a more poetically correct but
theatrically less exciting 11/10 syllables

▼ [4] Ff and most modern texts = 'Nor', Qq = 'Now'

113

| Hotspurre | I can no longer brooke thy Vanities. |

[Fight]
ENTER FALSTAFFE

| Falstaffe | Well said Hal, to it Hal. |

Nay you shall finde no
80   Boyes play heere, I can tell you.

ENTER DOWGLAS, HE FIGHTS WITH FALSTAFFE, WHO FALS DOWN
AS IF HE WERE DEAD. [1] **THE PRINCE KILLETH PERCIE**

| Hotspurre | Oh Harry, thou hast rob'd me of my youth : |

     I better brooke the losse of brittle life,
     Then those proud Titles thou hast wonne of me,
     They wound my thoghts worse, then the [2] sword my flesh :
85   But thought's the slave of Life,[3] and Life, Times foole ;
     And Time, that takes survey of all the world,
     Must have a stop.
                 O, I could Prophesie,
     But that the Earth,[4] and the [5] cold hand of death,
90   Lyes on my Tongue :   No Percy, thou art dust
     And food for ——— [6]

| Prince | For Wormes, brave Percy. |

                     Farewell [7] great heart :
     Ill-weav'd Ambition, how much art thou shrunke?
95   When that this bodie did containe a spirit,   L 72 - b
     A Kingdome for it was too small a bound :
     But now two paces of the vilest Earth
     Is roome enough.
                This Earth that beares the [8] dead,
100   Beares not alive so stout a Gentleman,
     If thou wer't sensible of curtesie,
     I should not make so great [9] a shew of Zeale.

L 72 - b / R 72 - b :   5. 4. 74 - 95

SD [1] most modern texts add a stage direction here for the exit of Dowglas

▼ [2] Q1 - 4 and most modern texts = 'thy', Q5/Ff = 'the'

▼ [3] Q2 - 5/Ff = 'But thought's the slave of Life', most modern texts = 'But thoughts, the slaves of life', taking this reading from Q1's 'But thoughts the slave of life'

▼ [4] Q1 most modern texts = 'earthy', Q2 - 5/Ff = 'Earth'

▼ [5] Qq most modern texts omit 'the', which is set by Ff

SD [6] most modern texts add a stage direction here for Hotspurre's death

▼ [7] most modern texts follow Qq and set 'Fare thee wel', Ff = 'Farewell'

▼ [8] Qq/Ff = 'the dead', some modern texts = 'thee dead'

▼ [9] some texts follow Q1 and set 'deare', Q2 - 5/Ff = 'great'

114

But let my favours hide thy mangled face,
And even in thy behalfe, Ile thanke my selfe
For doing these fayre Rites [1] of Tendernesse.

Adieu, and take thy praise with thee to heaven,
Thy ignomy [2] sleepe with thee in the grave,
But not remembred in thy Epitaph. [3]

What?
                    Old Acquaintance?
                                    Could not all this flesh
Keepe in a little life?
                    Poore Jacke, farewell:
I could have better spar'd a better man.

O, I should have a heavy misse of thee,
If I were much in love with Vanity.

Death hath not strucke so fat a Deere to day,
Though many dearer in this bloody Fray:
Imbowell'd will I see thee by and by.

Till then, in blood, by Noble Percie lye.

[Exit]
FALSTAFFE RISETH UP

Falstaffe   Imbowell'd? if thou imbowell mee to day, Ile
give you leave to powder me, and eat me too to morow.

[4] 'Twas time to counterfet, or that hotte Termagant Scot,
had paid me scot and lot too.
                                Counterfeit?
                            [5] I am no coun-
terfeit; to dye, is to be a counterfeit, for hee is but the
counterfeit of a man, who hath not the life of a man: But
to counterfeit dying, when a man thereby liveth, is to be
no counterfeit, but the true and perfect image of life indeede.
                The better part of Valour, is Discretion; in the
which better part, I have saved my life.

[W][1] at least one modern text follows Q1 and sets 'rights', most modern texts follow Q2 - 5/Ff = 'Rites'

[W][2] Q1 - 3/F3/most modern texts = 'ignominy', Q4 - 5/F1 - 2 = 'ignomy'

[SD][3] here most modern texts set a version of the Qq stage direction, 'He spieth Falstaffe on the ground'

[O][4] most modern texts follow Qq and set the oath omitted by Ff, 'Zbloud'

[W][5] modern texts follow Q1 - 4 and add 'I lie', omitted by Q5/Ff

¹ I am affraide of

135   this Gun-powder Percy though he be dead.

How if hee

should counterfeit too, and rise?

² I am afraid hee would

prove the better counterfeit: therefore Ile make him sure:

140   yea, and Ile sweare I kill'd him.

Why may not hee rise as

well as I: Nothing confutes me but eyes, and no-bodie

sees me.

Therefore sirra, with a new wound in your thigh

145   come you along³ me.

        [Takes Hotspurre on his backe]
    ENTER PRINCE AND JOHN OF LANCASTER

Prince   Come Brother John, full bravely hast thou flesht
    thy Maiden sword. ⁴

[Prince] John   But soft, who⁵ have we heere?

    Did you not tell me this Fat man was dead?

150   **Prince**   I did, I saw him dead,
    Breathlesse, and bleeding on the ground: Art thou alive?

    Or is it fantasie playes upon our eye-fight?

    I prethee speake, we will not trust our eyes
    Without our eares. ⁶

155   Thou art not what thou seem'st.

Falstaffe   No, that's certaine: I am not a double man: but
    if I be not Jacke Falstaffe, then am I a Jacke: There is Per-
    cy,⁷ if your Father will do me any Honor, so: if not, let him
    kill the next Percie himselfe.

160   I looke to be either Earle or
    Duke, I can assure you.

R 72 - b : 5. 4. 121 - 143

⁰₁ most modern texts follow Qq and set the oath omitted by Ff, 'Zounds'

⁰₂ most modern texts follow Qq and set the oath omitted by Ff, 'by my faith'

▼₃ Qq/F3/most modern texts set 'with', omitted by F1 - 2

ᵛᴾ₄ Ff set the opening of the line with a small 't' on 'thy', thus suggesting the speech is prose: Qq and most modern texts capitalise 'Thy' thus setting the speech as verse: this also allows [Prince] John's reply to combine with the second line as a line of split verse: if Ff remain as set, then the opening relaxation of the two brothers quickly turns into more formal language at the surprising (and ridiculous?) sight of the supposed dead Falstaffe lugging the dead Hotspurre on his back

▼₅ Q1 and most modern texts = 'whom', Q5/Ff = 'who'

?ˢᵀ₆ this could be set as between one and three sentences

ˢᴰ₇ most modern texts add a stage direction here that Falstaffe puts (throws?) Hotspurre down

Prince	Why, Percy I kill'd my selfe, and saw thee dead.
Falstaffe	Did'st thou?

                Lord, Lord, how the [1] world is given

165   to Lying?

                I graunt you I was downe, and out of Breath,
and so was he, but we rose both at an instant, and fought
a long houre by Shrewsburie clocke.

                            If I may be belee-

170   ved, so : if not, let them that should reward Valour, beare
the sinne upon their owne heads.

                          Ile take't on [2] my death
I gave him this wound in the Thigh : if the man were a-
live, and would deny it, [3] I would make him eate a peece

175   of my sword.

Prince John as **John**	This is the strangest Tale that *e're I heard.
Prince	This is the strangest Fellow, Brother John. R 72 - b

              Come bring your luggage Nobly on your backe :
    [4] For my part, if a lye may do thee grace,

180   Ile gil'd it with the happiest tearmes I have.

A RETREAT IS SOUNDED

              The Trumpets sound Retreat, the day is ours :
Come Brother, *let's to the highest of the field,
To see what Friends are living, who are dead.

[Exeunt]

Falstaffe	Ile follow as they say, for Reward.

185   Hee that rewards me, *heaven reward him.

                              If I do grow great again, [5]
Ile grow lesse?

                    For Ile purge, and leave Sacke, and live

190   cleanly, as a Nobleman should do.

[Exit]

R 72 - b / L 73 - b : 5. 4. 144 - 165

[1] Q1 and most modern texts = 'this', Q5/Ff = 'the'

[2] Qq and most modern texts = 'Ile take it upon', Ff = 'Ile take't on'

[3] most modern texts follow Qq and set the oath omitted by Ff, 'zounds'

[4] most modern texts indicate the Prince speaks this as an aside to Falstaffe

[5] most modern texts follow Qq and omit 'again', which is set in Ff

Scæna Quarta

[because of the earlier alteration, most modern texts list the new scene as #5]

THE TRUMPETS SOUND.
ENTER THE KING, PRINCE OF WALES, LORD JOHN OF LANCASTER,
EARLE OF WESTMERLAND, WITH WORCESTER &
VERNON PRISONERS

King	Thus ever did Rebellion finde Rebuke.	
	Ill-spirited Worcester, did we not [1] send Grace,	
	Pardon, and tearmes of Love to all of you?	
	And would'st thou turne our offers contrary?	
5	Misuse the tenor of thy Kinsmans trust?	
	Three Knights upon our party slaine to day,	
	A Noble Earle, and many a creature else,	
	Had been alive this houre,	
	If like a Christian thou had'st truly borne	
10	Betwixt our Armies, true Intelligence.	
Worcester	What I have done, my safety urg'd me to,	L 73 - b
	And I embrace this fortune patiently,	
	Since not to be avoyded, it fals on mee.	
King	Beare Worcester to [2] death, and Vernon too:	
15	Other Offenders we will pause upon.	

[Exit Worcester and Vernon]

How goes the Field?

Prince	The Noble Scot Lord Dowglas, when hee saw	
	The fortune of the day quite turn'd from him,	
	The Noble Percy slaine, and all his men,	
20	Upon the foot of feare, fled with the rest ;	
	And falling from a hill, he was so bruiz'd	
	That the pursuers tooke him.	
	At my Tent	
	The Dowglas is, and I beseech your Grace. [3]	
25	I may dispose of him.	
King	With all my heart.	

---

[1] Qq and most modern texts = 'not we', Ff = 'we not'

[2] Qq and most modern texts set 'the', which Ff omit

[3] F1 alone sets a period here, Qq/F2 and all modern texts either show no punctuation or set a comma

Prince	Then Brother John of Lancaster,
	To you° this honourable bounty shall belong: ° 1

Go to the Dowglas, and deliver him
30   Up to his pleasure, ransomlesse and free:
His Valour ² shewne upon our Crests to day,
Hath taught us how to cherish such high deeds,
Even in the bosome of our Adversaries.

∞ ³

King   Then this remaines: that we divide our Power.

35   You Sonne John, and my Cousin Westmerland
Towards Yorke shall bend you, with your deerest speed
To meet Northumberland, and the Prelate Scroope,
Who (as we heare) are busily in Armes.

My Selfe, and you Sonne Harry will towards Wales,
40   To fight with Glendower, and the Earle of March.

Rebellion in this Land shall lose his way,⁴
Meeting the Checke of such another day:
And since this Businesse so faire is done,
Let us not leave till all our owne be wonne.

[Exeunt]

FINIS

LS 1   Qq/Ff's irregular setting of this passage (8/12 syllables) makes enormous dramatic sense, for the pause
allows a moment before the enormous noble act (of defiance to the King?) is spoken on the longer line: the
modern restructuring to a regular passage of poetry (10/10) completely destroys the moment

W 2   most modern texts follow Q1 - 3 and set the plural 'Valours' in this line with the corresponding verb 'Have'
to start the next: Q4 - 5/Ff = the singular 'Valour', with the corresponding verb 'Hath'

Q 3   most modern texts set two lines for [Prince] John from Q1 - 4 which are not shown in Q5/Ff, viz.
                    I thanke your grace for this high curtesie,
                    Which I shall give away immediatly.

W 4   Q1 - 4 and most modern texts = 'sway', Q5/Ff = 'way'

119

APPENDIX A
THE UNEASY RELATIONSHIP OF FOLIO, QUARTOS, AND MODERN TEXTS

Between the years 1590 and 1611, one William Shakespeare, a playwright and actor, delivered to the company of which he was a major shareholder at least thirty-seven plays in handwritten manuscript form. Since the texts belonged to the company upon delivery, he derived no extra income from publishing them. Indeed, as far as scholars can establish, he took no interest in the publication of his plays.

Consequently, without his supervision, yet during his lifetime and shortly after, several different publishers printed eighteen of these plays, each in separate editions. Each of these texts, known as **'Quartos'** because of the page size and method of folding each printed sheet, was about the size of a modern hardback novel. In 1623, seven years after Shakespeare's death, Heminges and Condell, two friends, theatrical colleagues, actors, and fellow shareholders in the company, passed on to the printer, William Jaggard, the handwritten copies of not only these eighteen plays but a further eighteen, of which seventeen had been performed but not yet seen in print.[1] These thirty-six plays were issued in one large volume, each page about the size of a modern legal piece of paper. Anything printed in this larger format was known as 'folio', again because of the page size and the method of sheet folding. Thus the 1623 printing of the collected works is known as **the First Folio,** its 1632 reprint (with more than 1600 unauthorised corrections) the Second Folio, and the next reprint, the 1666 Third Folio, added the one missing play, *Pericles* (which had been set in quarto and performed).

The handwritten manuscript used for the copies of the texts from which both Quartos and the First Folio were printed came from a variety of sources. Closest to Shakespeare were those in his own hand, known as the 'foul papers' because of the natural blottings, crossings out, and corrections. Sometimes he had time to pass the material on to a manuscript copyist who would make a clean copy, known as the 'fair papers'. Whether fair (if there was sufficient time) or foul (if the performance deadline was close), the papers would be passed on to the Playhouse, where a 'Playhouse copy' would be made, from which the 'sides' (individual copies of each part with just a single cue line) would be prepared for each actor. Whether Playhouse copy, fair papers, or foul, the various Elizabethan and Jacobean handwritten manuscripts from which the quartos and Folio came have long since disappeared.

The first printed texts of the Shakespeare plays were products of a speaking-hearing society. They were based on rhetoric, a verbal form of arranging logic and ar-

---

[1] Though written between 1605–09, *Timon of Athens* was not performed publicly until 1761.

gument in a persuasive, pleasing, and entertaining fashion so as to win personal and public debates, a system which allowed individuals to express at one and the same time the steppingstones in an argument while releasing the underlying emotional feelings that accompanied it.[2] Naturally, when ideas were set on paper they mirrored this same form of progression in argument and the accompanying personal release, allowing both neat and untidy thoughts to be seen at a glance (see the General Introduction, pp. xvi–xxi). Thus what was set on paper was not just a silent debate. It was at the same time a reminder of how the human voice might be heard both logically and passionately in that debate.

Such reminders did not last into the eighteenth century. Three separate but interrelated needs insisted on cleaning up the original printings so that silent and speaking reader alike could more easily appreciate the beauties of one of England's greatest geniuses.

First, by 1700, publishing's main thrust was to provide texts to be read privately by people of taste and learning. Since grammar was now the foundation for all writing, publication, and reading, all the Elizabethan and early Jacobean material still based on rhetoric appeared at best archaic and at worst incomprehensible. All printing followed the new universality of grammatical and syntactical standards, standards which still apply today. Consequently any earlier book printed prior to the establishment of these standards had to be reshaped in order to be understood. And the Folio/Quarto scripts, even the revamped versions which had already begun to appear, presented problems in this regard, especially when dealing in the moments of messy human behaviour. Thus, while the first texts were reshaped according to the grammatical knowledge of the 1700s, much of the shaping of the rhetoric was (inadvertently) removed from the plays.

Secondly, the more Shakespeare came to be recognized as a literary poet rather than as a theatrical genius, the less the plays were likely to be considered as performance texts. Indeed plot lines of several of his plays were altered (or ignored) to satisfy the more refined tastes of the period. And the resultant demands for poetic and literary clarity, as well as those of grammar, altered the first printings even further.

Thirdly, scholars argued a need for revision of both Quarto and Folio texts because of 'interfering hands' (hands other than Shakespeare's) having had undue influence on the texts. No matter whether foul or fair papers or Playhouse copy, so the argument ran, several intermediaries would be involved between Shakespeare's writing of the plays and the printing of them. If the fair papers provided the source text,

---

[2] For an extraordinarily full analysis of the art of rhetoric, readers are guided to Sister Miriam Joseph, *Shakespeare's Use of the Arts of Language* (New York: Haffner Publishing Co., 1947). For a more theatrical overview, readers are directed to Bertram Joseph, *Acting Shakespeare* (New York: Theatre Arts Books, 1960). For an overview involving aspects of Ff/Qq, readers are immodestly recommended to Neil Freeman, *Shakespeare's First Texts*, op. cit.

a copyist might add some peculiarities, as per the well documented Ralph Crane.[3] If the Playhouse copy was the source text, extra information, mainly stage directions, would have been added by someone other than Shakespeare, turning the play from a somewhat literary document into a performance text. Finally, while more than five different compositors were involved in setting the First Folio, five did the bulk of the printing house work: each would have their individual pattern of typesetting—compositor E being singled out as far weaker than the rest. Thus between Shakespeare and the printed text might lie the hand(s) of as few as one and as many as three other people, even more when more than one compositor set an individual play. Therefore critics argue because there is the chance of so much interference between Shakespearean intent and the first printings of the plays, the plays do not offer a stylistic whole, i.e., while the words themselves are less likely to be interfered with, their shapings, the material consistently altered in the early 1700s, are not that of a single hand, and thus cannot be relied upon.

These well-intentioned grammatical and poetic alterations may have introduced Shakespeare to a wider reading audience, but their unforeseen effect was to remove the Elizabethan flavour of argument and of character development (especially in the areas of stress and the resulting textual irregularities), thus watering down and removing literally thousands of rhetorical and theatrical clues that those first performance scripts contained. And it is from this period that the division between ancient and modern texts begins. As a gross generalisation, the first texts, the First Folio and the quartos, could be dubbed 'Shakespeare for the stage'; the second, revamped early 1700 texts 'Shakespeare for the page'.

And virtually all current editions are based on the page texts of the early 1700s. While the words of each play remain basically the same, what shapes them, their sentences, punctuation, spelling, capitalisation and sometimes even line structure, is often altered, unwittingly destroying much of their practical theatrical value.

It is important to neither condemn the modern editions nor blindly accept the authority of the early stage texts as gospel. This is not a case of 'old texts good, so modern texts bad'. The modern texts are of great help in literary and historical research, especially as to the meanings of obscure words and phrases, and in explaining literary allusions and historical events. They offer guidance to alternative text readings made by reputed editors, plus sound grammatical readings of difficult passages and clarification of errors that appear in the first printings.[4] In short, they can

---

[3] Though not of the theatre (his principle work was to copy material for lawyers) Crane was involved in the preparation of at least five plays in the Folio, as well as two plays for Thomas Middleton. Scholars characterise his work as demonstrating regular and careful scene and act division, though he is criticised for his heavy use of punctuation and parentheses, apostrophes and hyphens, and 'massed entry' stage directions, i.e. where all the characters with entrances in the scene are listed in a single direction at the top of the scene irrespective of where they are supposed to enter.

give the starting point of the play's journey, an understanding of the story, and the conflict between characters within the story. But they can only go so far.

They cannot give you fully the conflict within each character, the very essence for the fullest understanding of the development and resolution of any Shakespeare play. Thanks to their rhetorical, theatrical base the old texts add this vital extra element. They illustrate with great clarity the 'ever-changing present' (see p. xvi in the General Introduction) in the intellectual and emotional life of each character; their passages of harmony and dysfunction, and transitions between such passages; the moments of their personal costs or rewards; and their sensual verbal dance of debate and release. In short, the old texts clearly demonstrate the essential elements of living, breathing, reacting humanity—especially in times of joyous or painful stress.

By presenting the information contained in the First Folio, together with modern restructurings, both tested against theatrical possibilities, these texts should go far in bridging the gap between the two different points of view.

---

[4] For example, the peculiar phrase 'a Table of greene fields' assigned to Mistress Quickly in describing the death of Falstaffe, *Henry V* (Act Two, Scene 3), has been superbly diagnosed as a case of poor penmanship being badly transcribed: the modern texts wisely set 'a babbled of green fields' instead.